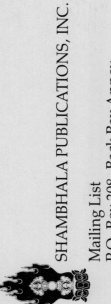

SHAMBHALA PUBLICATIONS, INC.

Mailing List
P.O. Box 308, Back Bay Annex
Boston, Massachusetts   02117

*If you wish to receive a copy
of the latest Shambhala Publications catalogue of books
and to be placed on our mailing list
please send us this card.*

PLEASE PRINT

Book in which this card was found
_____

NAME
_____

ADDRESS
_____

CITY & STATE
_____

ZIP OR POSTAL CODE   COUNTRY
_____
                    (IF OUTSIDE U.S.A.)

THE CHINESE ART OF TEA

John Blofeld

SHAMBHALA / BOSTON / 1985

SHAMBHALA PUBLICATIONS, INC.
314 Dartmouth Street
Boston, Massachusetts 02116

9 8 7 6 5 4 3 2 1
First Shambhala Edition
Printed in the United States of America
Distributed in the United States by Random House
and in Canada by Random House of Canada Ltd.

Library of Congress Cataloging in Publication Data
Blofeld, John Eaton Calthorpe, 1913-
    The Chinese art of tea.
    Includes index.
    1. Tea—China. I. Title.
GT2907.C6B58   1985   394.1'2   84-23661
ISBN 0-87773-320-1 (pbk.)
ISBN 0-394-73799-7 (Random House: pbk.)

Design/Eje Wray & Cheryl Craft
Typesetting/The Type Galley/Boulder CO in Linotron Trump

Frontispiece:
Detail from a
handscroll by Yu Ch'iu
entitled 'Scholars'
Picnic'.

Cover illustration:
"Scholars in a
Garden," from the
collection of The
Nelson-Atkins
Museum of Art,
Kansas City, Missouri
(Nelson Fund).
Reproduced by
permission.

To my tea brother Li Fêng-Hsing (pen name Yü-Yü),
to whom I am deeply grateful for warm encouragement
as well as for the rich mine of valuable material
provided by his tea books

Contents

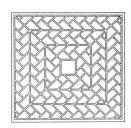

Millions of people all over the world enjoy drinking tea, but few are conversant with its long and colourful history. Emperors and peasants, Taoist recluses, Buddhist monks, wandering physicians, mandarins (the scholar-officials of old China), lovely ladies, craftsmen, potters, poets, singers, painters, architects, landscape gardeners, nomadic tribesmen who bartered horses for bricks of tea, and statesmen who used tea to buy off would-be invaders have all played their part in it. And tea in return, besides rewarding us with its flavour, aroma and pleasantly stimulating properties, has been considerably responsible for the development of the world's loveliest ceramics—whether in China, Japan, Korea, Dresden or Staffordshire!

All tea in the world came originally from China. Indeed, it is only in the last century and a half that tea has been grown (from Chinese seeds) anywhere outside that country, apart from some neighbouring realms where its history is much longer. Its close on 2,000-year-old story is therefore a fascinating part of Chinese culture.

Chinese tea lovers never developed an intricate tea ceremony like *chanoyu* in Japan—which, by the way, they tend not to like because its elaborate stylisation is quite contrary to the Taoistic feeling of spontaneity and carefree informality they associate with tea drinking. Nevertheless, there is definitely a Chinese art of tea. It is known as *ch'a-shu.*

Ch'a-shu embraces skill in the growing and processing of tea leaves; knowing how to brew fine teas so as to extract the maximum flavour and aroma; cultivating a taste for all kinds of delightful (but not necessarily expensive) ceramics and other accessories; collecting old poems, songs and stories about everything to do with tea; and, above all, knowing how to relax and savour a brew in pleasant surroundings so that a tea session becomes a short retreat from the stresses and strains of modern life. Additional aspects, rare because they involve large expense, are the building of a personal teahouse and the landscaping of the surroundings to make a perfect setting. Naturally, few people acquire a full knowledge of all these components. For everyday purposes, the important elements of the art are the following.

Tea is at its best when enjoyed in pleasant surroundings, whether indoors or out, where the atmosphere is tranquil, the setting harmonious. A large party is distracting, whereas the company of two or three relaxed and friendly people contributes to the enjoyment of unusually fine tea. This book provides all the information needed for procuring high-quality teas and making a choice among them, as well as for brewing tea expertly. The other two essentials are very pure water and a set of tea-things that please the eye on account of their subdued, unostentatious beauty, thus adding to the prevailing atmosphere of tranquil harmony. Nevertheless, a perfect combination of these five—setting, company, tea, water and tea-things—will fail to work its magic in the absence of the special attitude required to do them justice.

The key to that attitude is mindfulness. The world today is so full of distractions that mindfulness, which must have come about spontaneously in times gone by, has to be cultivated. Once this has been achieved, a thousand hitherto unnoticed beauties will reveal themselves. For example, there is music in the hiss and bubble of a kettle, a springtime freshness in the fragrance of the steam rising from the teacups, and a gentle exhilaration—too subtle to be apparent to a distracted mind—results from certain mysterious properties inherent in the tea itself, particularly in the case of green and oolong teas as opposed to black teas.

When the mind, having freed itself from the trammels of past and future, is fully concentrated on the Here and Now, a whole range of pleasures involving ears, eyes, nose, palate and mood can be enjoyed by two or three people who have come together to make and drink fine tea. However, that enjoyment would fade in the presence of reverential silence, stiff formality or self-consciousness. One should be comfortably relaxed and behave with perfect naturalness, talking of this and that. To the Chinese way of thinking, the observance of the "do's and don'ts" required for the Japanese tea ceremony is foreign to the benign spirit of tea. If one chooses to talk about the beauty of the tea-things and the setting, well and good; but there should be no feeling of being obliged to do so. Chinese votaries of the tea art often have a fund of tea poems and tea anecdotes on which to draw, but again there is no obligation to channel the conversation in that direction. The spirit of tea is like the spirit of the Tao: it flows spontaneously, roaming here and there impatient of restraint.

If one happens to have no interest in philosophical or metaphysical matters, talking learnedly about them while drinking tea becomes ridiculous. On the other hand, those who like that sort of thing may be gladdened by the reflection that the art of tea, like most traditional Chinese (and Japanese) arts, involves harmony among the Three Powers—heaven, earth and man. Heaven provides the sunshine, mist and rain needed for growing tea; earth provides soil to nourish the tea plants, clay from which all kinds of ceramic tea-things can be fashioned and rocky springs overflowing with pure water with which to brew the tea. To these man adds the skills by which processed tea leaves, water and ceramics are conjoined to create the fabric of a seductive art. The special role played in the art's development by Taoist recluses and Buddhist monks demands a chapter to itself.

The carefree spirit essential to the Chinese art of tea is well exemplified by an ancient song with which Tea Master Chang T'ieh-Chün concludes his contemporary tea book. Inspired by that happy ending, I have made a loose translation with which to open mine:

Life is Meant for Happiness

Life is full of ups and downs;
Sunshine comes and goes;
Then why such fuss and bustle?
Let's live for happiness.
Why care what people say,
Since ups and downs are fleeting
And everything's uncertain?
Take autumn harvests,
Moonlight on the river,
Once gorgeous mansions
Falling into ruin,
Fame, great wealth and honour—
All of them ephemeral,
Like pearling frost or dew;
For all depend on fate.
Away with worldly cares!
Why dream of splendid mansions
Or care for name and fame?

When free, sing songs or strum
Some charming melodies.
When you meet good fortune,
Then make the most of it.
Invite your choicest friends
To picnic by the water,
Have fun with lute or chess,
Appraise choice books and paintings,
Or fish beneath the willows,
Go boating with some pretty girls,
Tell happy-ending stories
Or tales of ancient happenings.
Enjoy the rich embroidery
Of leaves and perfumed blossom.
Echo the birdsong on your lute.
Let others treat you as they will
With feelings warm or cold.
Draw water from a spring
Beneath the blue-green pines
Boil it on an earthen stove
Surrounded by bamboos.
With Dragon-and-Phoenix tea leaves.
Make a delicious brew,
Then taste the joys
Of Lu T'ung's seven bowls*
Of famous Yang-Hsien tea!

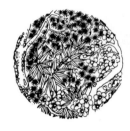

*The significance of the famous 'seven bowls', known to every Chinese votary of the tea art, is dealt with fully in Chapter 1.

It is my great hope that this first attempt at an English language Chinese tea book will appeal not just to tea lovers, but to all who like to read nostalgically about the departed splendours of imperial China. These splendours linger only in books, but now that the new regime is coming to regret the passing of so much that was unique in the ancient traditions it is possible to hope that some at least will be revived. Already the tradition of drinking Dragon's Well tea made with clear water from Tiger-Run Spring has returned. Among the countless visitors to Hangchow's West Lake many climb to the spring to enjoy this memorable pleasure. Perhaps some readers of this book will swell their numbers!

JOHN BLOFELD

Wu-Wei Chai
Studio for Letting-things-happen-of-themselves
House of Wind and Cloud
1983

Acknowledgements

I wish to express my profound indebtedness to the authors of the Chinese tea books listed in the notes—most especially 'Yü Yü' (Mr. Li Fêng-hsing), upon whose fund of tea legends I have drawn heavily. I am also deeply grateful to Mr. Stephen Batchelor, who took immense trouble to gather information on tea drinking in Korea; to his Korean informants, the Venerable monks Pŏpchŏng Sŭnim, Kyongbong Sŭnim, Sonbae Sŭnim, Mr. Han Ungbin and others; to Ms. Terese Tse Bartholomew of the Asian Art Museum, San Francisco, for her knowledgeable article on I-Hsing porcelain; to Mr. and Ms. Wong Hong-Sze of Singapore, Dr. J.C. Covell and Mr. S.H.G. Twining, a director of the famous British tea firm of that name, for sending me valuable materials in English; and to Mr. Hsü Wu-pen and Mr. Hsieh Hsi-chin of Hong Kong for presenting me with a collection of Chinese language tea books.

Warm gratitude is also due to those who kindly provided many of the illustrations, namely: the Percival David Foundation of

Chinese Art, London University; the Nelson Gallery, Kansas City, Missouri; Dr. Rayson Huang, Vice-Chancellor of the University of Hong Kong; Mr. David Abotomey, who kindly made a special series of drawings to illustrate various types of tea utensil; Mr. Ratchasak Gertpu, who photographed some of my tea-things; and Ms. Ursula Smilde, who spent long hours searching London's museums and foundations for paintings to illustrate the book. For some reason, although Chinese literature on tea is prolific there seem to be very few extant paintings of people enjoying tea, so the London search proved to be somewhat of a wild-goose chase; but I am nonetheless grateful to Ursula for her prodigious efforts and to the curators of various museums and foundations for giving her very generous co-operation.

Introduction

As an aid to the enjoyment of the histories, poems and anecdotes in this book the necessary background information has been assembled below.

Ruled by the 'Son of Heaven,' the hereditary monarch whose powers were in theory virtually unlimited, the Chinese Empire was in actual fact largely governed by a scholarly élite. The selection of this élite was surprisingly democratic, as anybody who managed to do well in several successive state examinations became eligible for senior posts ranging from county magistrate up to the highest ministers of state. The curriculum centered on history, philosophy, statecraft and ethics (all cast in a Confucian mould) as well as poetry, essay-writing and calligraphy. Consequently these scholar-officials were well versed in the formal literary arts and could mostly write good poetry, play music and paint attractive landscapes. They were expected to cherish high Confucian ideals and be incapable of corruption, injustice or folly. However, being human, they ranged in practice from

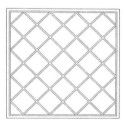

The Traditional Background

men of the highest integrity to venal rascals, from sensitive poets to self-satisfied pedants. As each of the great dynasties arose in turn and soared to its zenith—a state of affairs usually covering about two centuries—scholars entrusted with the administration would tend to be admirable people, but gradually the vigour of the reigning dynasty would be sapped by luxury. Then the imperial family and great ministers would fall prey to the blandishments of a multitude of palace eunuchs, whereupon venality among officials high and low would rise unchecked; a century or more might pass before the scholars and peasants grew desparate enough to revolt in favour of a new dynasty. I imagine that even in the darkest times the scholar-officials, whether corrupt or not, were often engaging personages whose erudition, literary talent and graceful demeanour would charm their acquaintances, no matter whether they were saints or rogues.

As for the state religion that the officials were bound to uphold, this was a type of Confucianism which, while accepting a largely impersonal moral order as inherent in the workings of the universe, fostered no clearly defined belief in gods or an afterlife and thus amounted to agnosticism. State and clan rituals in honour of ancestral spirits were meticulously performed, but more on account of the salutary influences these solemn rites exercised on public order than because they reflected any particular religious conviction. There was nothing to hinder officials from subscribing to the exalted mystical doctrines of Taoism or Buddhism, but that was a private matter unlikely to affect their public conduct to an appreciable extent.

The ordinary people, however, put their faith in a *mélange* of several religions, making a colourful hotchpotch of the cult of ancestors, Confucianism, Buddhism, Taoism and—especially if their education were limited or nonexistent—a nameless system of folk beliefs stemming from remote antiquity. These last related to immeasurably vast heavenly regions as well as to whole galaxies of deities, plus nature spirits, goblins, sprites, ghosts, were-tigers, demons and so on. This folk religion, though lacking a mystical or ethical basis, was vivid

and satisfying, for many of those supernatural beings were credited with powers to cure disease, avert misfortune and generally make life more tolerable. Of special importance to the more fanciful tea stories are the so-called Immortals. It was popularly believed that men and women skilled in Taoist arts could so transmogrify themselves that their flesh became a jade-like substance impervious to fire and ice. These beings were capable of flying wherever they wished, so some resided in splendid cloud palaces, while others went off to live in P'êng-Lai (the Isles of the Blessed) in the Eastern Ocean and yet others in a paradise located somewhere in central Asia; many, however, chose to continue living as hermits in China's hills and mountains where, according to a host of stories, they occasionally had intercourse with mortals and attracted disciples eager to be transmogrified in their turn.

Many votaries of the art of tea, coming mostly from the scholar class, shared the near-agnosticism of their confrères and did not ascribe spiritual values to that art. However, for reasons to be explained, Taoists and Buddhists, who had originally prized tea drinking as a means of retaining alertness during meditation, were often involved in the growing—and even the processing—of tea, so a fair number of famous Tea Masters came from their ranks and influenced the evolution of the tea art, as will appear from appropriate passages in this book.

Other Relevant Information

CHINESE TEA

In this book, the word 'tea' usually signifies Chinese tea—not the strong reddish-brown infusion that needs milk and sugar to make it palatable; nor yet the costly China teas (such as lapsang souchong) dispensed on cedar-shaded lawns by Edwardian hostesses, their faces half-hidden by enormous floppy hats; nor yet the coarse tea commonly provided in Chinese restaurants; but the hundreds of varieties of fine-quality tea grown for Chinese tea lovers. Several teas of this kind are becoming increasingly available in the West. They belong to three categories: green (unfermented), semi-green (partially fermented tea generally called 'oolong' in English) and red (fermented tea called 'black tea' in English). 'China tea' is a term used for tea grown for the foreign market; 'Chinese tea' refers to that grown primarily for local consumption.

TEA GARDENS   This term denotes not open-air places for drinking tea but tea estates.

VESSELS   *Chien* were wide, shallow bowls used in ancient times both for infusing and drinking tea. They are also sometimes called saucers.

Bowls, which were used to the same two purposes at a later date, were usually somewhat larger than a modern rice bowl of the kind used instead of a plate when one eats with chopsticks.

'Cups' were (and are) usually smaller than those commonly used by Western peoples, besides being handleless and without saucers.

'*Chung*' are somewhat larger cups, equipped with lids and saucers but handleless. They can be used like ordinary teacups, or the tea can be both steeped and drunk in them.

DYNASTIES

Pre-T'ang	(dynasties before AD 618)
T'ang	618-907
Sung	960-1280
Yüan (Mongol)	1264-1348
Ming	1368-1644
Ch'ing	(Manchu) 1644-1912

Two of these overlap because rival dynasties, old and new, coexisted for a few decades. Some have gaps between them, during which minor dynasties flourished or else the Dragon Throne remained unoccupied.

The Chinese Art of Tea

Tea in History and Legend

Though the art of brewing tea certainly evolved in China, nobody is sure when it began. Ch'an (Zen) followers humorously credit Bodhidharma with the genesis of tea, but no knowledgeable person takes this seriously. The Indian monk who introduced the Zen form of Buddhism into China around AD 520 is said to have cut off his eyelids so as not to fall asleep during meditation. The legend goes on to say that where they fell a plant called *ch'a*, with leaves shaped like eyelids, sprang up and provided meditators with a means of staving off sleep. As a matter of fact, tea was drunk several centuries before Bodhidharma's time.

Popular belief credits the discovery of the properties of tea to the divine Emperor Shên Nung (2737-2697 BC), the so-called 'father of agriculture' who according to legend experimented with many hundreds of herbs; but this is surely myth rather than history. Around the time of Confucius, (the sixth century BC), a herb called *t'u* was regularly used in funeral offerings. The Chinese character for this plant resembles that for *ch'a* (tea) and is often confused with it, but

Pre-T'ang Period (Before AD 618)

Chinese tea men affirm that *t'u* is in fact what is nowadays sometimes called 'bitter tea'—a herb botanically unrelated to the tea family. However that may be, it can be confidently stated that tea was known in the Three Kingdoms epoch (AD 222-277). During the Six Dynasties epoch (AD 386-589), the habit of tea drinking spread rapidly in the south and more slowly in the north of China. We may suppose, then, that the first concoction of tea was brewed very early in the Christian era, if not before; but it was not until the glorious T'ang dynasty that the art of tea came into being and took its place side by side with painting, calligraphy, poetic composition, lute-playing, *wei-chi*,* the martial arts, incense appreciation parties, landscape gardening and other scholarly pastimes.

*a kind of chess played with 360 pieces

T'ang Dynasty (618-907)

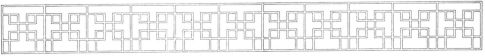

Tea, originally drunk for its medicinal properties, had already become popular as a beverage in court circles by early T'ang times; and we may judge that the habit quickly spread to all classes of the people as it was soon taken up by the Mongol, Tartar, Turkish and Tibetan nomads living north and west of China's frontiers. Indeed, it soon became essential to the nomads' diet, for their food consisted wholly of meat and dairy products; tea, drunk in copious quantities, was found to be a satisfactory remedy for ills resulting from the lack of vegetables and fruit. As for what may properly be called the art of tea, this was instituted by an individual subsequently styled the 'Tea God.'

The 'Tea God', Lu Yü

Throughout the ages certain people in China were elevated posthumously, either by imperial decree or by popular acclaim, to divine rank. It was believed that this honour, bestowed by no less a personage than the reigning Son of Heaven, or by the acclaim of the 'black-haired' people generally, carried such weight in the heavenly regions that the recipients did in fact become gods and live forever in the vast and shining courts of heaven. To achieve this status a person had to prove himself a model of excellence or a benefactor of the human race. Such a one was the eighth-century Lu Yü, who wrote the first comprehensive work on tea, known as the *Ch'a Ching* or *Tea Classic.*

What has been officially recorded of his life is sparse; but, supplemented by hearsay, the story makes good reading. He was born in Hupei Province, central China. Nothing is known about his parents, who seem to have abandoned him as a tiny boy by the riverside. Happily, Ch'an (Zen) Master Chi Ch'an, abbot of Dragon Cloud Monastery, found and adopted the child, to whom he gave the name Lu Yü, taken from the text attached to line six of hexagram fifty-three (*Chien:* 'gradual progress') in the *I Ching* or *Book of Change:* 'The wild goose moves gradually towards the *mainland (Lu).* Its *feathers (yü)* can be used for ritual purposes—good fortune!' Alas, the boy was unmoved by the mystical doctrines of Zen, for he preferred the more statesman-like teaching of Confucius. His adoptive father therefore put him to work cleaning the monastic lavatory (a useful but degrading punishment now favoured by the Chinese Communists) and looking after a herd of thirty cattle rescued from butchery which had been presented to the temple as an act of merit. Even so, the child's Confucian zeal for learning triumphed over these difficulties, as is borne out by an account of him sitting astride an ox and practising calligraphy with a stick on the animal's neck! After a time boredom induced him to run off with a group of strolling players. Though by no means handsome and further handicapped by an impediment of speech, he was welcome on account of his excellent sense of humour and skill in cutting and

editing the texts of plays, perhaps, too, he already showed signs of becoming an accomplished musician, a poet and an authority on everything to do with tea.

Later he settled in Chekiang Province, then as always renowned for its scholars, where his gifts won for him a nominal post that carried with it a theoretical responsibility for the literary output of the heir to the Dragon Throne! The last decades of his long life were spent in semi-seclusion polishing his writings, particularly the famous *Tea Classic*, which was to establish him as the first of the great Tea Masters.

The *Tea Classic* begins with a statement—surprising these days, when tea is largely culled from low shrubs—that tea plants vary from one or two feet high to much more than ten feet, and that in Szechuan Province there are tea trees of such girth that two men with outstretched arms are barely able to embrace the trunk! The contents of the work include descriptions of tea trees and their habitats, the instruments required for processing the leaves, the utensils used for infusing and serving tea, the places where the purest of pure water can be found, the characteristics of numerous varieties of tea, and much else besides. I once translated a handwritten copy of this work but made no attempt to publish it, for little of the information it contains is relevant to the art as it is developed in subsequent dynasties. The *Tea Classic* is a curiosity rather than a useful source of information for present-day tea lovers. Moreover, several delightful tea books came to be written in the centuries that followed and such books are still being written today.

Of the stories told about Lu Yü there is one that points to his almost miraculous ability to distinguish subtle differences when judging the relative purity of various kinds of water used for making tea. Before effective water-purifying methods had been evolved, such an ability was esteemed as an important component of the Tea Master's art. We are told that while voyaging down the Yangtze River as the guest of a high-ranking dignitary, Master Lu Yü was invited to taste a jar of water which his host had ordered to be drawn from the midstream of the river at Nanling, where the water was reputed to be 'the finest under heaven.' Taking an experimental sip, Lu Yü put down his ladle in disgust, declaring it to be low-grade water drawn from close to the river bank, where, of course, it might be polluted or brackish. 'Oh no!' cried the officer responsible for bringing it. 'A hundred witnesses can testify that I personally drew this water in midstream at Nanling, as His Excellency ordered!' Whereupon Lu Yü put a second ladleful to his lips and announced: 'Well, it could be Nanling mainstream water, but it has been heavily diluted with water drawn from near the river bank.' Overawed by this percipience, the officer confessed that some of the precious water had slopped out of the jar during the sudden rocking of the little boat hired to convey it to the mandarin's ship, so he had topped it up with water drawn from the place where the boat had been moored when the loss occurred. 'Ah, Master Lu!' cried the rueful officer, 'you are clearly an Immortal!'

Another story does honour to his adoptive father, the abbot of Dragon Cloud Monastery, who seems to have welcomed him back after his wanderings with the strolling players. The abbot was so fond of tea prepared by Lu Yü that when the latter left home for the second time he gave up tea drinking altogether, either from grief or because nobody else could prepare tea exactly as he liked it. By chance, this singular affair came to the ears of the Son of Heaven, who refused to believe that Master Lu's skill was beyond emulation. To put this opinion to the test he commanded that the abbot be summoned to the capital and brought before him. As though to pay special honour to the old monk, the Emperor had his guest's tea brewed by a court lady whose expertise was held to be unrivalled. As the abbot respectfully raised the cup, the Lord of Ten Thousand Years remarked: 'Your Reverence will surely find this tea as good as if it had been brewed by your son.' But the abbot, having taken a sip, gently put the tea bowl down.

'Ha,' said the emperor to himself, 'this charlatan is just showing off. We'll soon unmask him!' For Master Lu had also been summoned to the palace and ordered to brew tea for the emperor's unnamed guest. This tea being brought in, the old monk, unaware that his adopted son was in the palace, sipped and smiled delightedly. 'Your Majesty!' he cried, 'this tea is superb! Even my son could not better it!' By now convinced of the old man's amazing power of discernment, the Son of Heaven brought father and son together and witnessed their joyful reunion.

It is clear that Master Lu, though impatient of the efforts made to rear him as a Buddhist, really loved his adoptive father, for on receiving news of the latter's death he wept for days on end and wrote a poem suggestive of tender feeling. It ran:

I have no longing for golden cups,
Nor yet for goblets of white jade,
Nor for dawning light upon the plains
Or evening sun behind the hills.
What I long and long and long for
Is water from the river flooding from Chingling!

The last line implies: 'Much as I prize the water drawn from pure mountain springs, I would gladly drink tea made from common water if it flowed from the place where my father used to live.'

Our general picture of Master Lu is that of an eccentric yet lovable man, but there is just one horribly discordant note. An ancient record states laconically: 'Lu Hung-chien (one of Lu's several names), having picked some tea across the river, ordered a serving boy to watch over its firing. The boy fell asleep; the leaves were charred. Hung-chien furiously fastened him in a wire cage and threw him into the fire!' There is no way of knowing what truth, if any, is to be found in this story. One can only hope it was sheer fabrication, for otherwise Tea Master Lu would scarcely deserve a place among the gods.

Tea, while still wild and scarce, was culled not from bushes but from tall trees growing in the shadow of high mountain peaks. Originally used medicinally, or to ward off sleep or as an antidote to the effects of too much rich food and alcohol, it became increasingly prized for its flavour and for the beauty of tea accessories. During T'ang times it was held that the best tea came from Yang-Hsien, which is situated in a mountainous region on the borders of Kiangsu and Chekiang Provinces (not very far from the modern Shanghai), so with the growth of tea cultivation much of that region was taken over by tea gardens. At the end of the eighth century an imperial envoy sent to investigate conditions there was presented by a mountain-dwelling monk with some of the Yang-Hsien tea which Lu Yü had lauded as the finest of all. The envoy immediately dispatched a thousand ounces of it to court, which responded by demanding an annual supply. This was the origin of the 'tribute tea' that was destined to become so vitally important to the Chinese economy. The annual quantity of tribute tea soon rose to thousands of catties* of which the choicest was reserved for the Son of Heaven's own use and the next best for his thousands of palace ladies and members of the imperial family, the rest being bestowed on high officials. Throughout the T'ang and successive dynasties the quantity rose by leaps and bounds, causing hardship to peasants in the tea areas (cultivation having spread to several provinces); but it benefited the economy as a whole and gave a powerful impetus to development of the ceramic arts besides playing a role in the defence of frontier regions.

> *1 catty = roughly 1⅓ lb

By the end of the eighth century 30,000 people were involved in picking and firing tribute tea during a period of thirty days each year. Selecting a lucky day in the third moon,* tea officials assembled in a temple on the slopes of Mount Ming-Ling and made sacrifices to the mountain deity. Thereafter a whole army of tea pickers, mostly girls, would be sent up the slopes in the early morning, their movements

> *approximately April

controlled by red signal flags. Picking stopped at noon. During the remainder of each day the leaves would be fired, in other words dried in a special roaster, then powdered and pressed into a paste which would be put into moulds and kept there till it hardened into a cake before being packaged and sent off. This processing had to be completed by sunset. At selected villages in the area, besides a large gathering of officials, caterers and so on there would be officially and privately owned wine shops and temporary buildings housing pleasure girls and singers. A poem runs:

In the mountains, wine and song,
Joy camps full of charming ladies
—Girls and wine unlimited.
Where else can one find such music
Or wine and dine so sumptuously?

Evidently, the pleasure girls were unusually attractive: the rustics must have been overwhelmed. Nevertheless, for them hardship was inevitable as labour for the tribute tea was exacted during the ploughing season and the workers were poorly paid by officials who guarded public funds jealously and were probably corrupt as well. Though the annual product was 18,000 catties (24,000 lb), the cultivation of the rice fields suffered and such wages as were earned by the peasants were largely spent on those pretty girls. To make matters worse, private trade in tea was forbidden, so the cultivators could not easily make money on the side. On the other hand, people living in the selected villages just described must have benefited from such places' rapid expansion into market towns.

The 'Tea Doter', Lu T'ung

The second great figure in the history of tea was Lu T'ung, a poet who is said to have loved tea as much as life itself. Born in North China towards the end of the eighth century, he lived a secluded life on Cottage Mountain in Hunan Province under the name Master Jade Spring. Both as a poet and a Tea Master he won the admiration of some of the greatest scholars in the land. He seems to have subscribed to the Taoist principle of *wu-wei* (no calculated activity, just spontaneous action in accordance with one's nature) for from morning to night he scarcely did anything else but intone poems and brew the beverage on which he doted so extravagantly that some of his contemporaries thought him daft. The ebullience of his enthusiasm can be gauged from a line in one of his poems: 'I care not a jot for immortal life, but only for the taste of tea.' However, he is best remembered as the author of the most famous of all tea poems, which is entitled 'Thanks to Imperial Censor Mêng for his Gift of Freshly Picked Tea.' Unable to translate it in a manner that does it real justice, I can but offer a semi-metric rendering.

*The surnames of the 'Tea God' and the 'Tea Doter' are written differently in Chinese

The Song of Tea

I was lying lost in slumber as the morning sun climbed high,
When my dreams were shattered by a thunderous knocking at the door.
An officer had brought a letter from the imperial censor,
Its three great seals slanting across the white silk cover.
Opening it, I read some words that brought him vividly to mind.
He wrote that he was sending three hundred catties of moon-shaped cakes of tea,
For a road had been cut at the year's beginning to a special tea garden—
Such tea! And plucked so early in the year, when insects had scarcely begun their chatter,
When spring breezes had just begun to blow
And spring flowers dared not open,

1

As the emperor still awaited
The annual toll of Yang-Hsien tea!

2   *Ah, how wonderful that tea, plucked ere the kindly breeze*
Had swept away the pearling frost upon its leaves
And the tiny leaf-buds shone like gold!
Being packed when fresh and redolent of firing,
Its essential goodness had been cherished, instead of wasted.
Such tea was intended for the court and high nobility;
How had it reached the hut of a humble mountain-dweller?

3   *To honour the tea, I shut my brushwood gate,*
Lest common folk intrude,
And donned my gauze cup
To brew and taste it on my own.

4   *The first bowl sleekly moistened throat and lips;*
The second banished all my loneliness;
The third expelled the dullness from my mind,
Sharpening inspiration gained from all the books I've read.
The fourth brought forth light perspiration,
Dispersing a lifetime's troubles through my pores.
The fifth bowl cleansed ev'ry atom of my being.
The sixth has made me kin to the Immortals.
This seventh is the utmost I can drink—
A light breeze issues from my armpits.

5   *Where are those Isles of Immortals whither I am bound?*
I, Master Jade Spring, will ride upon this breeze
To the place where the Immortals alight upon the earth,
Guarded by their divinity from wind and rain.
How can I bear the fate of countless beings
Born to bitter toil amid the towering peaks?

I must ask Censor Mêng if he can tell
Whether those beings will ever be allowed to rest.

I have arbitrarily divided the poem into five numbered stanzas for convenience in explaining points that may seem obscure. The first stanza contains three matters that require explanation. Firstly, imperial censors were high officials whose duty it was to brave the emperor's wrath even at the cost of putting their lives in jeopardy whenever there was need to admonish him for notable misconduct. Secondly, at the time of the T'ang dynasty tea leaves were pounded, crushed and made into a paste that was pressed into moulds before being packed to await infusion: hence 'cakes of tea.' Finally, the spring flowers 'dared not open' because, officially, spring could not begin until the emperor had received the first batch of tribute tea. The second stanza emphasizes that tea is at its best if plucked while young and tender. Stanza three implies that tea of such quality deserved great reverence. Stanza four is so delightful in the original that most Chinese tea lovers know it by heart. The bowls referred to were wooden bowls larger than modern teacups, so the amount required to fill seven might well be as much as even a 'tea doter' could manage to drink at a sitting. The latter part of stanza five reveals that Lu T'ung had a deep sympathy for the thousands of tea pickers who slaved away harvesting the leaves from trees growing on precipices high up in the mountains. The picking had to be done prior to dawn when, in early spring, the mountain weather could be cold, for tea picked after dawn has less fragrance. Besides, all picking stopped at noon so the girls had to work arduously from about four in the morning until then in order to gather the great quantities required by the Dragon Throne.

Seen in this light, the earlier part of stanza five proves to have a double meaning. No doubt the effects of those seven bowls of exquisite tea *did* make Lu T'ung feel as though he had sprouted the wings of an Immortal. However, the lines also imply: 'The only people who normally receive a share of the tribute tea live in palaces or great mansions, guarded by their high status from all discomfort—how different their state from that of the peasants who toil to harvest it!'

In the Palace Museum, Taiwan, there is a painting of Lu T'ung by the late Sung artist Ch'ien Hsien which shows him seated with two companions on a carpet in the open air waiting for the kettle to boil. The expression on their faces is, as my tea brother says, like that of people assembled to witness the birth of a Buddha or Messiah! Alas, this joyous Tea Master's life ended in unexpected tragedy. He had gone on a visit to the capital at the invitation of two great ministers of the Emperor Wên Tsung. That monarch, finding himself being treated by his army chiefs as a puppet, had secretly ordered the civilian branch of the government to arrange for the ambush and destruction of the regiment of guards. Somehow the secret leaked out. The enraged guards slaughtered not only the 600 soldiers preparing to overpower them but also some 2,000 members of the loyal ministers' families and their supporters. During this holocaust the luckless 'Tea Doter' had his head smitten from his body and exposed in public like that of a malefactor.

CURIOSITIES OF THE PERIOD

In T'ang times, as we have seen, tribute tea took the form of caked leaves. Though tea was available to ordinary people in four forms—coarse, loose-leaf, powdered and caked—most tea drinkers preferred the caked form, cutting off small slabs which were then powdered with a special instrument to make it ready for infusion. As kettles had not yet been evolved, a kind of earthenware bottle was used to boil the water. Tea Masters, who were very fussy about the exact temperature of the water or 'soup' as it was called, were unable to see the size of the bubbles (as one can by lifting the lid of a kettle), so they judged the temperature by the sounds made by the seething water. The term 'soup' was used because various strong-tasting ingredients such as onion, ginger, orange peel or peppermint were often brewed up with the water. Instead of teacups, bowls were used. These were originally of wood but later of pottery, of which that from Yüeh-Chou (now called Yü-Yao) was fashionable. In rich households, teapots and drinking vessels were sometimes made of chased gold or silver, but subsequently the use of metal was frowned upon by Tea Masters.

During the ninth century two Japanese monks returning to their country took some tea seeds home. This was the genesis of Japanese tea. No doubt they had been staying in monasteries where powdered tea, of the kind still used in the Japanese tea ceremony, was commonly used.

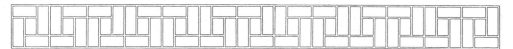

Sung Dynasty (960-1280)

After the T'ang, much of China was ruled for a time by Tartar invaders. However, in the year 960 a new dynasty, the Sung, came near to equalling the T'ang in splendour. The art of tea rose to new heights, having received encouragement from the Emperor Hui Tsung (1101-1125), the third most important figure in the story of tea.

The 'Tea Emperor', Hui Tsung

This monarch, though shockingly careless of his duties as a ruler, was a likeable and erudite personage whose treatise on tea, the *Ta Kuan Ch'a Lun**covers the subject so expertly that many doubt whether a Son of Heaven dwelling in august isolation from his people could be the real author; yet there is firm evidence that he was. Indeed, he was more of an artist than a ruler, excelling in poetry, essay-writing and painting besides having a temperament so touchingly romantic that his obsession with wine, women and song finally cost him his Dragon Throne!

*see Chapter 2

Within the palace precincts Emperor Hui Tsung had no fewer than 3,912 ladies (his empresses, concubines and female attendants), but even this great variety of beauty failed to satisfy his longings.

A Sung dynasty ceramic bowl with silver rim and rabbit's-fur glaze pattern. See page 172.

While on a semi-incognito visit to the willow lanes housing the dwellings of beautiful and accomplished courtesans, he succumbed to the charms of Li Shih-Shih, perhaps the most famous of that sisterhood in Chinese history. Exiling her lover, he flouted the conventions of the imperial household by admitting a non-virgin to the rank of concubine. Unfortunately, this lovely lady led him even deeper into debauchery. To the stupefied amazement of the traditionalists, he opened a department store within the palace walls and staffed it with the ladies of the 'Great Within'! For the first time in history ministers of state found themselves buying rare delicacies from beauties upon whom it would previously have cost them their lives to gaze! Doubtless the wines and teas tasted all the more delightful on account of this novel circumstance.

Not surprisingly, conditions of anarchy gradually engulfed his poorly governed empire. The Son of Heaven's consequent abdication in favour of his son failed to avert a fearful retribution. Discontent seethed to a point where a horde of Tartars invaded the capital and carried off both Hui Tsung and his reigning son to exile in the melancholy wilderness beyond the Great Wall. There they languished in captivity until death released them. Hui Tsung left behind a poignant poem, which runs:

I still recall the splendours of my jade-like capital,
My home as ruler of those boundless territories,
The Forest of Coral and the Hall of Jade,
The morning levees, the evening music.
Now the people of that beauteous city
Have fled its lonely solitude.
How remote were those youthful dreams of mine
From this sad Mongolian wilderness!
Ah, where are the hills of my homeland?
I must bear the cacophony of barbarous flutes
Blowing piercingly among the plum blossom.

Poor, poor emperor—how he must have enjoyed drinking tea in his Forest of Coral and Hall of Jade! As an erstwhile monarch he must have loathed those nine long years of exile, especially as there was no tea to drink apart from coarse brick tea, salted and churned with camel's butter to suit the palates of nomadic Tartars!

Sung Tribute Tea

The many delicious teas produced to this day in South China's Fukien Province, though barely known in T'ang times, became the main source of tribute tea under the Sung from 976 onwards. The finest kind took the name Pei-Yüan from that of the most famous of the forty-six imperial tea gardens, each with its own furnaces and processing units. It was gathered at the time known as Excited Insects (the beginning of March), such tea being at its best if picked when covered with morning dew. The pickers, controlled by drum and cymbal signals, had to work in the chilly hours preceding dawn, the quality of the leaves being more highly valued than the quantity. These highly trained girls wore labels so that tea thieves could not mingle with them unnoticed; their nails had to be kept neither short nor long, for nails (not fingers) were used for plucking so as to avoid sweat and body-heat contamination. All the girls had baskets strapped to their backs. Some carried pitchers of water for the frequent washing of fingernails; others stood nearby with full pails for freshening up the newly picked leaves.

After dawn came grading into five classes, namely 'small bud,' 'medium bud' (with a single leaf on each stalk), 'purple bud' (with two leaves on a stalk), 'two leaves with bud' and 'stem tops.' The first two became tribute tea, the rest being sold on the market by the authorities. Then came steaming, rolling, drying, grinding, pressing the leaf paste into metal moulds and roasting in an oven. This last was done repeatedly over a period of from six to twelve days, after which the tea was cooled immediately by vigorous fanning. Of the thirty-six grades the finest were conveyed by relays of fast horses to the capital so as to be completely fresh on arrival. The values of the top grades were

1. beyond price,
2. two ounces of gold,
3. one ounce of gold and
4. half-ounce of gold per cake

the cakes being small enough to hold in the palm of the hand. The Wu-I Mountains where it grew remain the source of the best teas in the world.

Although tribute tea remained in the form of caked tea, loose-leaf tea such as we use today was already gaining popularity. The preferred source of tea leaves had changed; so had the favoured sources of pure water. Trade with the tribes on the fringes of the empire had become so important that tea, normally bartered for horses from the steppes, could also be used to control those wild nomads. If they grew turbulent their annual tea quota would be withheld. To be sure of having stocks large enough to procure all the horses for the army, the government for a time prohibited all those below the rank of a seventh-grade mandarin from buying tea. Even so, a shortage of tea was one of the reasons why the border tribes revolted and set up an independent state in the northern part of the empire!

Sung ceramics, widely used as tea accessories, remain one of the wonders of the world. Tea bowls had given place to wide, shallow vessels often called 'saucers' for which the Chinese name is *chien*. The best, which came from Fu-an in Fukien Province, were purplish black with lines like a rabbit's fur. As many Sung connoisseurs favoured a whitish tea leaf, black utensils were used to enhance by contrast the colour of the tea. Some tea votaries used gold, silver, iron or bamboo spoons with which to spoon the tea leaves into the water, whereas later Tea Masters frowned on the use of metal. The 'soup' bottle had not as yet been supplanted by the kettle.

The Tea Commissioner, Ts'ai Hsiang

Another great tea man of Sung times was the scholar-official Ts'ai Hsiang. Born in 1012, he lived to the age of fifty-six. As a young man he passed with honours the highest state examination, after which he rose to be a notable statesman in addition to becoming a famous Tea Master. As a native of Fukien Province he had ample opportunity to learn about tea and was given for a time the post of tea commissioner, whose duties were to supervise the picking, processing, packing and transport of tribute tea. Furthermore, he composed the *Ch'a*

Lu, a tea record written specially for the emperor's perusal. Thanks to him and other scholars of his calibre, the art of tea reached its apex of refinement under the Sung.

Small Rounds, the special tea he selected for tribute, was manufactured from a variety of leaf known as Small Leaf Dragon, which after being crushed and pounded was moulded into unusually small round 'cakes.' Its excellence was such that the tiny quantity reaching the market was worth two ounces of gold per catty (one and a half ounces of gold per pound)—an exorbitant price even now, let alone nine hundred years ago! On one occasion an important personage invited Ts'ai Hsiang to come and taste a rare tea of which a few spoonfuls had somehow come into his possession. By chance an unexpected guest appeared and was privileged to join the party. No sooner had Commissioner Ts'ai taken a sip than he remarked: 'Excellency, I fear you have been duped. This really is Small Rounds, but it has been adulterated with a tea of lower quality.' In some amazement the host questioned his servant, who fell to his knees and confessed: 'There was just enough of the special tea to serve two people, so when the second honoured guest arrived, I was obliged to add a small quantity of Big Rounds tea.' Clearly, Ts'ai's palate was unusually delicate!

During his term as Governor of Fukien, Ts'ai visited the Nêng-Jên Monastery, whose abbot owned some tea trees growing in a mountain crevice. From their leaves he had manufactured eight cakes of tea, of a kind later to be known as Stone Cliff White. Four were given to Governor Ts'ai; the other four were sent without Ts'ai's knowledge to a noted scholar and resident of the capital surnamed Wang. A year or so later Ts'ai happened to visit Wang, who, to honour so great a Tea Master, ordered his people to serve the finest tea in his possession. On tasting it, Ts'ai exclaimed: 'How strange! This tea most surely comes from Nêng-Jên Monastery in my own faraway province. How did you manage to get it?' Wang asked a servant to find out where the tea had come from, and discovered that Ts'ai had not been mistaken. Full of admiration, he declared the commissioner to be the greatest tea expert in the world!

Commissioner Ts'ai enjoyed tea contests, a pastime popular among high officials during T'ang and Sung but thereafter rarely practised. Having nominated a judge, each contestant in turn would brew a tea of his choice with pure water brought from heaven-knows-what mountain spring. On one occasion, this great Tea Master actually lost! How was that possible? Well, although his competitor's brand of tea was inferior to Ts'ai's, the brew was superb because he had used what an old Sung record terms 'bamboo-strained water'. No one living now knows precisely what that means, but the record stands.

Another story about the tea commissioner is unrelated to tea but classed as a tea story because he figures as its protagonist. To understand its full impact on a Chinese audience one has to imagine how it would be if a Western raconteur were to bring together a ridiculously incongruous set of divine beings such as Jove, the Virgin Mary, Thor, Satan and Krishna! According to his story Commissioner Ts'ai, as Governor of Fukien, set about constructing a bridge over an important water route near Ch'uan-Chou which was destined to become known as 'The Best Bridge Under Heaven'. This much is historical fact; the rest quite obviously spurious. With this preface, the tale goes back to mythical times.

Some 30,000 years ago the Pole Star deity, on attaining immortality, cut his body open, drew out his intestines and threw them into the Lo River, where, as their essential *ch'i* (life force) was not dispersed, they became a tortoise spirit and a snake spirit. Over the centuries these spirits, by absorbing quantities of sun and moon essence, acquired the art of assuming human form. Pretending to be ferrymen, they regularly sank their boat in mid-river and gobbled up their passengers, but there came a day when a voice from heaven cried: 'You have on board a distinguished scholar surnamed Ts'ai. Do not harm him!' In fact, a pregnant lady in the bows was carrying the future tea

commissioner in her womb. Grateful for heaven's intervention, she vowed that her baby should one day build a bridge so that no more people would be drowned. Years later Ts'ai set out to fulfil this promise, but tides kept sweeping in from the sea and washing away the bridge before its completion. The goddess Kuan-Yin, recognising that those spirits were responsible, rode off to the bridge site on an auspicious cloud, fashioned a largish boat from a bamboo leaf, co-opted the local river god as boatman and, assuming the form of a beautiful maiden, announced to the bystanders her willingness to marry any youth who could throw a golden coin accurately enough to touch her body. Should coins fall into the boat without touching her, however, they would be used towards paying for the completion of the new bridge.

The news spread far and wide. Within two days hundreds of golden coins lay in the boat, but none had reached its goal. Meanwhile, the Taoist Immortal Lü Tung-Pin decided to tease the goddess. Taking the form of a youthful scholar, he flung a coin that touched her sacred person. But the goddess instantly recognised him and lodged a complaint with the Jade Emperor, ruler of the Taoist heavens. Accordingly, the thunder god was commanded to strike the impious immortal and destroy him, so poor Tung-Pin fled to the house of a young scholar, changed himself into a small insect and hid in the young man's writing brush. The thunder god, knowing that the scholar was destined for fame, dared not hurl his lightning. For failure to fulfil his mission, he was banished. Moreover the luckless scholar, instead of attaining high honours at the age of twenty-two, had to wait a further sixty years before being able to pass the final examination.

The governor now composed a letter to the Dragon King asking him to select an auspicious day for continuing construction. Summoning his staff, he inquired which of them was capable of going under the sea to deliver a letter to the Dragon King's palace. By chance, one of his juniors was a youth called Hsia Ta-Hai, a name identical in sound to the Chinese phrase for 'Go under the sea'. Thinking the governor had said 'Whichever of you is Hsia Ta-Hai will deliver the letter', he tremblingly asked to be excused, but the governor firmly handed him the letter and went out to dinner.

Poor Hsia, realising that drowning would be preferable to the penalty for disobeying a direct order, got as drunk as 'a lizard pickled in alcohol' to mitigate the pain of drowning and then obediently went off to perform his hopeless task. However, on reaching the beach he collapsed and lay there snoring.

Came the dawn. On regaining his senses, Hsia felt for the official package tucked in his bosom and found it smaller! Opening his robe, he discovered a missive bearing the Dragon King's seal, so he rushed back to hand the governor what proved to be a sheet of paper bearing the single character *ts'u* ('vinegar'), written in vermilion ink. From the shape of the character the governor deduced that it indicated the hour of the cock*on the twenty-first day of the month. The tools and materials needed were assembled in advance, and no sooner had the auspicious hour arrived than the tide ebbed, making it easy to sink the pillars. The rest of the project met with uninterrupted success. No one had ever seen a better bridge.

*5-7 PM

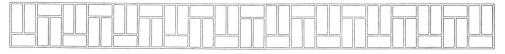

Ming Dynasty (1368-1644)

In a sense, the story of tea in China does not need to be carried any further than the Sung period; for although that dynasty came to an end some seven centuries ago little pertaining to the various ways of preparing and drinking tea has changed substantially since then, except for the widespread adoption of loose-leaf tea early in the Ming dynasty and its retention until now as the most widespread form. So the final part of this history can be dealt with more briefly.

After Sung, the Empire was ruled by Mongols for eighty-four years. Then arose the Ming dynasty, which sought to revive past glories. Under its rule a very important institution, the Horse and Tea Bureau, played a vital part in the economy. The demand for tea by the border tribes had become so great that it ranked as a commodity of major significance to the Empire, both militarily and financially. The Bureau, being responsible for the bartering of tea for horses, was put under the control of very high-ranking officials; and as an incentive to the people to grow tea in sufficient quantity to barter for all the horses needed, the tax was reduced to the moderate rate fixed during the T'ang dynasty, namely one-hundredth part of the crop. Otherwise, tea administration followed the Sung pattern.

It was in late Ming times that tea first reached Europe. Of those Europeans wealthy enough to afford it some were enthusiastic, but a rumour spread that tea weakened a person's vitality and was being exported to sap the energies of potential enemies of China! This curious belief strikes one as ironic, for a time would come when England, by forcing Indian opium on China, would indeed sap the energies of a people who should have been better rewarded for giving the whole world tea!

The tea art under the Ming dynasty closely reflected Sung traditions: its votaries, far from swilling tea in so-called 'thirsty ox fashion', liked to sip it delicately in accordance with the maxim 'Tea should be drunk often but in small quantities'. Meanwhile, great progress was made with the manufacture of ceramic accessories. The teapot remained in favour as the ideal utensil for brewing tea, as did the shallow drinking bowls called *chien* that were later to give way to cups. However, the kettle completely took over from the 'tea bottle'—a name henceforth transferred to a very different object, a ceramic canister for storing tea leaves.

Ch'ing or Manchu Dynasty (1644-1911)

Under Manchu rule, the Sung-Ming traditions were continued. However, the ancient tea tax was completely abolished in recognition that

An eighteenth century moulded and enamelled saucer depicting tea-making out of doors.

tea had become as necessary to the people as the traditional tax-free necessities: oil, salt, firewood, rice, soyabean sauce and vinegar. The elegance of tea accessories in the homes of the rich and their preoccupation with special kinds of water can be gauged from a passage in that enthralling eighteenth-century novel *The Dream of the Red Chamber*. A Buddhist nun serves tea to two of the main protagonist's friends using a pumpkin-shaped cup beautifully inscribed with minute calligraphy and a cup resembling a miniature begging bowl inscribed with 'pearl drop' script. The hero complains that a pure jade cup handed to him is unremarkable, so the little nun brings him a large bowl carved from a gnarled and ancient bamboo root 'in the likeness of a coiled dragon with horns like antlers'. When asked if the tea has been specially made with rainwater, the nun scornfully replies: 'Can you not tell the difference? How very disappointing! I made it with melted snow taken from the branches of a winter plum tree five years ago and have kept the snow water in a demon-green glaze jar. Only once before have I brought myself to sample such a treasure. Surely you can tell the difference? How could mere rainwater have such lightness or be used for a tea such as this one?'

The Diffusion of Tea Drinking to Other Countries

During the period of the Ch'ing dynasty tea drinking spread throughout the world, having already reached Japan and Korea during T'ang times. Seeds brought from China led to the establishment of a very profitable tea industry in India (1834) and Sri Lanka (around 1870), though the tea produced there is processed differently from Chinese tea in order to suit the non-Chinese purchaser's requirements. The fact that Anglo-Saxons generally add milk and sugar and consequently favour a stronger, darker brew may be due to an accident of history. Most Chinese dislike milk in any form and prefer an infusion of tea free from any additives. However, the Manchus, like the Mongols and Tibetans, often added butter or milk. It may be that eighteenth-century English travellers, being occasionally entertained by Manchu officials, came to like drinking tea with milk; in Stuart times, on the other hand, it had been drunk without additives in the Chinese fashion.

The Chinese written character for tea is generally pronounced *ch'a* but changes to *tei* in some coastal dialects. Hence *cha* (or *chai*) is the name still used in Russia, Central Asia and India, where the first consignments of tea came by overland routes from China; whereas most European countries call it 'tea', *thé* or by some similar name, indicating that the first consignments came from coastal ports in south-east China. The additives commonly used, besides milk and sugar, are: lemon and sugar (or even jam) in Russia and Central Asia, mint in many Muslim countries and spirits such as vodka or rum during the winter in very cold countries. Indians actually *boil* tea, while Burmese and Thais sometimes chew salted tea leaves. The Japanese, though they use powdered tea for their tea ceremony, normally drink unadulterated loose-leaf tea like the majority of Chinese, but the taste is dissimilar as it has been gradually modified to suit the palates of a people who were traditionally fish eaters.

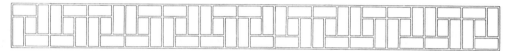

The Twentieth Century

The main changes affecting Chinese tea in modern times are: the development of northern and central Taiwan as a very important tea-producing region, which has occurred since the mainland became Communist; an increasing use of mechanical processing methods; and a notable decrease in tea drinking that has been due, in mainland China, to poverty and elsewhere to a growing preference for coffee. Coffee in East Asia is widely drunk in handsome decorated coffee shops with discreet alcoves, dim lighting and piped music that appeal to young people, who generally prefer this sort of Western ambience; besides, instant coffee, which has been on the market for many years, suits the rapid pace of modern life, and cola drinks have made big inroads. It remains to be seen whether such recent inventions as instant tea and tea bags will redress the balance. If they do, tea exporters will be pleased, but to many votaries of fine tea they are anathema!

During the first half of this century the use of tea as a thirst-quenching beverage, as an adjunct to social intercourse and as the focus of

BEFORE THE CHINESE COMMUNIST REVOLUTION

the tea art remained much the same in China as in Ming and Ch'ing times. It was drunk many times a day, but especially in the mornings, by rich and poor alike; indeed, Lao Shê's famous novel *Rickshaw Boy* reveals that rickshaw pullers, despite their poverty, drank it copiously. In almost every urban household there stood a large pot of tea kept warm in a padded basket, for it would have been unthinkable to have no tea on hand to offer whoever happened to drop in. Tea stores, fragrant with the piles of the fresh jasmine buds used in North China as an additive, and teahouses, with facilities to suit all purses, abounded. Tips and key money were called 'tea money'. There was hot tea in every hotel bedroom, bathhouses dispensed it to their customers as a matter of course, and so did a great many of the city's more affluent shops.

Ceremonial usages involving tea were manifold. They included offerings of tea to the gods and before the tombs of ancestors, to parents at betrothal ceremonies and to seniors by juniors at almost every kind of traditional social ceremony. At weddings tea was indispensable because, as tea trees live a hundred years or more if allowed to do so, and as they do not move from place to place, tea symbolises long life and marital fidelity. Nationalist government officials, following the Ch'ing dynasty precedent, sometimes had tea served to callers at the beginning of an interview; when the host raised his cup for the second time, the caller was expected to take the hint and leave. During Ch'ing times, no sooner did a mandarin finger his teacup for the second time than his subordinates would shout for the caller's conveyance to be brought round, without troubling to make sure that the polite dismissal had been accepted—it surely had!

As for the tea art prior to the Communist Revolution, it was still practised by many among the educated classes, as is the case in Taiwan and Chinese overseas communities to this day. Because the Chinese tea art is uncomplicated, in well-bred circles one could easily pick up the simple rules just by watching family members or friends enjoying it.

In Communist China, tea still plays its traditional role at official levels; moreover hot tea is served on trains and aeroplanes. Packets of excellent tea and vacuum flasks of very hot water are to be found in every bedroom of the better-class hotels. Famous teas such as Dragon's Well are still served in or near the tea gardens where they grow or in the vicinity of a few historically important mountain springs. But there the likeness to the old days ends. Sad to say, even quite ordinary tea is considered a luxury, so people have grown accustomed to drinking hot water—which they still *refer* to as tea—and may go for weeks at a time without a drop of real tea. Consequently, many youngsters have acquired no taste for it and often decline to drink it! I could not believe this of Chinese people had I not seen how it is with my own eyes. As for the once packed teahouses, in the Chinese cities I visited in 1982 I saw no teahouses at all, though I have heard they still exist in certain tea-growing regions. Especially in Canton and Peking, where in the old days a day that began without drinking morning tea at home or going to a teahouse was almost unheard of, the unimaginable has come to pass.

TEA IN MAINLAND CHINA TODAY

The Emperor Hui Tsung's Treatise on Tea

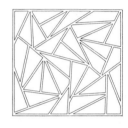

Though the original text of this ancient treatise, written in 1107, is not very long, it is a masterly piece of work—as indeed it should be, coming from the brush of such an exalted personage. Its interest for modern readers is threefold.

First, it ranks as a literary curiosity. It is extraordinary that a Son of Heaven living in virtual isolation from his people could be so knowledgeable about tea production. However, of the many hundred rulers who occupied the Dragon Throne in turn during a period of several thousand years, Hui Tsung (1101-1125) was assuredly the most scholarly and probably one of the most charming. When he composed this treatise, the *Ta Kuan Ch'a Lun*, his heart was serene, for the empire was at peace and no shadow of his impending exile in captivity* *see Chapter 1 had yet arisen.

Second, the treatise reveals the wide range of skills involved in the growing, processing, preparation, infusion and drinking of caked tea, thus enabling us to understand the delight taken by Sung courtiers and scholar-officials in the intricacies of the tea art as it was in those far-off days. The detailed instructions for infusing caked tea have little bearing on our manner of drinking tea today, but it is fascinating to learn how much effort was expended on ensuring that the liquid should be close to perfection as regards flavour, aroma and colour.

Third, some of the extracts from the treatise help us to understand the enthusiasm of the ancient tea votaries for a beverage at once so costly, so difficult to prepare and so richly productive of pleasures involving each of the sense organs.

In order to make the text easily understandable without recourse to a mass of footnotes the extracts are preceded by the following summary of the stages involved in processing and preparing caked tea in the ancient manner.

1   Before being dispatched to court the tea leaves had been plucked, steamed, crushed, fired and compressed into cakes by packing them in moulds under pressure. Each cake took the form of a solid wedge much too hard to be crumbled with one's fingers.

2   Preparing and drinking the infusion involved the following processes:

Using a very sharp instrument to slice off the required quantity of caked leaves;

Crushing them into a fine powder;

Passing the powder several times through a sieve;

Boiling pure water in a tall, narrow kettle somewhat like a bottle;

Putting the freshly powdered leaves into a *chien*, the saucer-like bowl used for infusing and drinking;

Pouring water from the kettle onto the leaves;

Whisking the infusion with a bamboo whisk vaguely reminiscent of a shaving brush, but with sharp-pointed bamboo slivers in place of bristles;

Drinking the infusion from the *chien* itself, but avoiding the sediment, much as one drinks Turkish coffee;

Several pourings of more water onto the rich sediment and drinking the renewed infusions;

Occasionally eating a part of the sediment remaining.

In the section entitled 'Water' we find that there were up to seven pourings of water on the caked tea in the *chien*. That the tea did not become insipid, as would certainly happen if leaves in a teapot were infused so many times, was due to the fact that the tea powder sank rapidly to the bottom after each whisking. Obviously, the tea that passed the drinker's lips as he sipped each bowlful was a lightish liquid which had absorbed only a small part of the goodness of the powdered leaves. As the water lay on them for such a short while after each pouring, the goodness slowly released by the congealed leaf powder at the bottom of the bowl lasted until the end.

3

    The emperor's introduction to his treatise covers the following points. People in those days, he tells us, were generally not appreciative enough of the beneficial effects produced by drinking properly prepared tea: namely that it induces lightness of spirit, clarity of mind and freedom from all sense of constriction, whether mental or physical; and that it promotes such serenity that mundane cares fall away so that whatever is strident or exacerbating in daily life can be put out of mind for a while. At the time of writing, the empire, he says, was prosperous, free from disturbances and well ordered. People of quality, having an abundance of everything they desired, were increasingly turning their minds towards such elegant pursuits as the tea art, with the result that the harvesting and processing of tea leaves, the quality of the final product and the skill required for its preparation had all reached optimum level. Such was the enthusiasm for enjoying tea, savouring its quality and vying with others in the matter of brewing it that even very ordinary people now thought it shameful to be ignorant about tea and the ways of enjoying it. The introduction ends with these words: 'When I am at leisure, I too like to go into all the intricacies of tea. I hardly suppose that with future generations it will be otherwise, so I have set down everything I know about tea in the twenty sections that follow.'

Extracts From The Treatise

All comments are the translator's

PLUCKING

Harvesting the leaves should begin well before day-break and stop shortly after. Picking must be done with the finger-nails, not with the fingers, lest the freshness and taste be contaminated . . . Leaves of whitish colour shaped like sparrows' tongues or grains of corn are best. One leaf per shoot is ideal; two leaves per shoot is next best; if there are more, the product will be inferior.

STEAMING & CRUSHING

This stage is immensely important to the excellence of the tea. Under-steamed leaves will be too light in colour and taste too strong. Over-steaming will break them up, darken their colour and cause them to emit a burnt odour.

OVERALL PROCESSING

Both leaves and implements should first be thoroughly washed. The amount of steaming and crushing should be exactly right. Grinding the prepared leaves into a paste requires heating, for which the fire must be of just the right strength and be supplied for precisely the right length of time.

Teas vary as much in appearance as do the faces of men. If the consistency of caked tea is not dense enough, the surface of the cake will be wrinkled and lack lustre, whereas it should be both glossy and close-knit. Caked tea processed on the day it was picked has a light purple colour; if the processing has taken longer, it will be darker. When caked tea is powdered ready for infusion, the powder will look whitish but turn yellow when infused. There are also fine tea pastes with a greenish colour; the powder, though grey, becomes white upon infusion. However, teas may look excellent and yet be rather poor, or look ordinary and nevertheless be remarkably good, so one should not go too much by appearances . . . Unfortunately tea merchants have many artifices for making tea look much better than it really is.

White tea is different from all others and deemed the finest. With wide-spreading branches and thin shiny leaves, the trees grow wild on forested cliffs. Their product is very sparse, however, and there is nothing one can do about it. Four or five families on the Pei-Yüan tea estate have some trees of this kind, but only a couple of them come into leaf, so no more than two or three bagfuls can be gathered each year. Both shoots and leaves are small; steaming and firing them is rather difficult; for if the temperature is not exactly right, they will taste like ordinary tea. Thus, a high order of skill is needed and the drying must be carefully done. If everything is exactly as it should be, the product of such trees will excel all others.

For powdering caked tea, the implement should be of silver or, at worst, of forged iron. Ordinary iron, being subject to rust, will ruin it . . . The sieving apparatus should be finely meshed and very strong; the tea leaves must trickle through it under their own momentum, for they must not be touched with the hand. Three sievings will ensure that the powder is very fine; even after two, it should be capable of floating on water, be glossy and have exactly the right colour.

MIXING
& DRINKING
VESSEL

The best kinds of chien (bowl) are very dark blue—almost black. They should be relatively deep so that the surface of the liquid will attain a milky colour, and also rather wide to allow for whipping with a bamboo whisk.

WHISK

This should be made of flexible bamboo; the handle should be heavy, the brush-like slivers light, their tips sharp as swords. Then, when the whisk is used, there are not likely to be too many bubbles.

'BOTTLE'

*This was a tall narrow type of kettle with a long, curved spout.

*The moistened powder coheres and becomes a paste, above which is the liquid which one drinks.

The bottle* should be made of gold or silver, its size just right. Correct pouring depends greatly on the spout. The orifice where the spout emerges from the 'bottle' should be wide; from there the spout should curve a lot and its lip be small and higher than the rest of the vessel, so that, when the water boils, none will be lost. If the bottle does not drip when pouring, the surface of the tea paste in the bowl will not be marred.*

WATER

There are several methods of mixing the hot water with the powdered tea . . . The following method produces wonderful results. One puts a suitable amount of powdered tea into a little hot water that has already been poured into the chien and mixes the two to form a paste; then one pours in more water, rotating the 'bottle' so as to distribute the pouring evenly.

COLOUR

Tea that turns white on infusion is best. Bluish grey is next best; greyish white comes third, and yellowish white fourth. If the weather was right when the tea was picked and the processing has been

*perfect, it will certainly be pure white; whereas if the weather was
too warm and the shoots had been growing so quickly that the
picking and processing could not be completed in time, even white
tea turns yellow. A bluish-grey colour indicates that the tea has
been insufficiently steamed and crushed; a greyish-white colour
results from too much steaming and crushing. If the processing has
been incomplete, the colour becomes too dark. Over-firing gives the
tea a reddish colour.*

The complete treatise covers absolutely everything that tea connoisseurs of that period should know about the beverage, from plucking and processing to drinking. This remarkable coverage is not apparent from the above extracts, for all technical details have been
omitted apart from those which strike me as being either picturesque
or important to our general understanding of the tea art in Sung
times. However, a desire to do justice to the memory of the scholarly
Emperor Hui Tsung impels me to reiterate that his knowledge of tea
was by no means limited to its aesthetic aspects. It is certain that this
Son of Heaven, fated to suffer for his dismal performance as a ruler,
would have been able to manage a tea garden and processing factory
with unprecedented expertise.

Sometimes, when drinking tea alone in reflective mood, I like to
fantasise about him. I am sure that somewhere within the depths of
his magnificent palace there was a small, rather unpretentious room
where the Lord of Ten Thousand Years experimented with fine teas,
brewing them in various manners with his own august hands. No
doubt such conduct was puzzling, and even shocking, to the horde of
palace ladies and eunuch attendants whose duty it was to bathe and
dress the emperor, wait upon him hand and foot and ensure that nothing remotely suggestive of manual labour—other than the wield-
ing of a writing brush or the Imperial chopsticks—ever came his way.

More than seven hundred years later, the Viceroy Li Hung-
Chang, while on a visit to England, was invited by Queen Victoria to

witness a tennis match. Obviously His Excellency enjoyed it immensely, for his head turned from side to side as he watched every movement of the ball. Later, he remarked: 'Truly, Your Majesty, it is an entrancing game. But, tell me, why do the courtiers not pay little boys to pat the balls to and fro on their behalf? That would save them so much unnecessary fatigue.'

This (to my mind sensible) remark can help us to appreciate the consternation aroused in palace circles by the knowledge that His Celestial Majesty sometimes insisted on brewing his own tea! I imagine, too, that those of the imperial ladies who, having attained to a high level of perfection in related skills, had the honour of preparing the monarch's tea must have been hard put to it to keep up the standard required by China's one and only 'Tea Emperor.'

A Ming Dynasty Tea Manual

The following extracts are taken from the *Ch'a Shu,* a manual or memorial to the throne composed by Hsü Tzê-Shu.* The sections omitted cover much the same ground as the emperor's treatise; those retained concern the how and where of actually drinking tea. By the time the manual was composed caked tea had given way to loose-leaf tea infused in a teapot and drunk from cups. It is interesting to note that the leaves were still thrown into a potful of boiling water instead of having the water poured over them. Otherwise, much of the advice given here is highly relevant to us today.

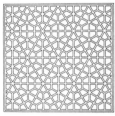

*also called Hsü Jan-Ming

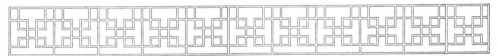

Have the utensils ready to hand and make sure that they are perfectly clean. Set them out on the table, putting down the teapot lid inner face upwards or laying it on a saucer. The inner face must not come in contact with the table, as the smell of lacquer or of food remnants would spoil the taste of the tea. After boiling water has

The Extracts

The notes are the translator's

INFUSION

been poured into the pot, take some tea leaves in your hand and throw them in. Then replace the lid. Wait for as long as it takes to breathe in and out thrice before pouring the tea into the cups, and then pour it straight back into the teapot so as to release the fragrance. After waiting for the space of another three breaths to let the leaves settle, pour out the tea for your guests. If this method is used, the tea will taste very fresh and its fragrance be delicious. Its effect will be to promote well-being, banish weariness and raise your spirit.

DRINKING

A pot of tea should not be replenished more than once. The first infusion will taste deliciously fresh; the second will have a sweet and pure taste; whereas a third would be insipid. So the quantity of water in the kettle should not be much. However, rather than have too little, there should be enough for some to be poured on the tea leaves after the second infusion, as it will continue to emit a pleasant aroma and can be used later for cleansing the mouth after meals.*

GUESTS

If one's guests are in a boisterous mood, it is better to give them wine to drink and, if they get somewhat tipsy, follow this up with a pot of very ordinary tea. It is only in the company of one's own kind, just those close friends with whom one can talk quietly about anything under the sun without formality, that one should call the serving boys to bring in the stove, fetch water and brew up some tea. The extent to which the serving of the tea is or is not completely informal will depend on the number of guests.

TEAROOM

Close to one's study, it is good to have a small tearoom, which should be spacious, clean, well lit and comfortable. Against the wall place two portable stoves, properly covered to stop the ashes from floating about in the air. Outside the tearoom there should be a wooden stand for the utensils in which water is stored and a small table for the various accessories, as well as a rack for hanging teacloths. *Those objects are brought into the room only when required. All should have covers to keep them free from dirt that might affect the tea. The charcoal heap should be located well away from the stoves and kept dry so that it will burn well. There should be enough space between stoves and wall to allow for frequent sweeping and, even more important, to guard against fire.*

Making tea and burning incense are elegant pastimes, so there is no objection to seeing to them oneself. However, when there are guests, they must not be neglected, so it is better to train a couple of young boys to deal with such matters. Every day they should clean the teathings, but never handle any of them without first asking the master's permission. When the boys have been busy making tea several times they should be allowed some time to rest and given a few cakes with a pot of tolerably good tea. The art of tea requires that attention be given to all sorts of things, both elegant and humdrum. No small detail should be neglected.

TEA BOYS

—In idle moments
—When bored with poetry
—Thoughts confused
—Beating time to songs
—When the music stops
—Living in seclusion
—Enjoying scholarly pastimes
—Conversing late at night
—Studying on a sunny day
—In the bridal chamber
—Detaining favoured guests
—Playing host to scholars or pretty girls
—Visiting friends returned from far away
—In perfect weather
—When skies are overcast

TIMES FOR DRINKING TEA

The original text of this section takes a near-poetic form and comprises twenty-four four-syllable lines.

—Watching boats glide past on the canal
—Midst trees and bamboos
—When flowers bud and birds chatter
—On hot days by a lotus pond
—Burning incense in the courtyard
—After tipsy guests have left
—When the youngsters have gone out
—On visits to secluded temples
—When viewing springs and scenic rocks

Tea Gardens

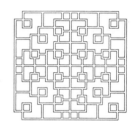

We have seen that tea in its wild state grows on great trees, some of which can be reached, if at all, only by arduous climbing in the high mountains. To this day, certain varieties are plucked from trees of mighty girth rising to a height of thirty feet or more. The famous Pu-Êrh tea grown in Yunnan Province is one of these. However, most tea now comes from tea gardens (tea estates, as we should call them) where the shrubs are pruned to a height not greater than four feet, so that plucking the leaves becomes relatively easy. The tea flowers are nipped in the bud to enable the leaves to receive more nourishment. At the age of ten years the shrubs should be stripped of their branches down to within one or two inches from ground level; for then, within three or four years, the new branches and leaves will be dense.

Plucking tea is a highly skilled task mostly performed by teams of girls, each numbering four or five. The finest crop is gathered in spring before the rains have swelled the tender leaves. Yet there are a few connoisseurs who prefer leaves plucked after the fall of winter snow. Known as Cloud-Ball tea, this unusual kind is green, sweet and deliciously fragrant. There are yet other eccentric connoisseurs who favour tea plucked when autumn frost arrives; this is known as dew tea. It would seem that early spring, autumn and winter are all propitious for harvesting. Teas plucked during the late spring rains are of somewhat inferior quality, but the yield is good. Those picked in summer, known as Yellow Branch teas, are decidedly of a lower quality. The ideal time of day for picking is during the hours before sunrise, when the natural fragrance is at its height. The tea girls have to leave their warm beds at two or three in the morning and brave the chill mountain winds, to say nothing of risking encounters with poisonous snakes and insects; so they sing as they climb, to keep up their spirits. That their simple peasant songs are not without charm can be judged from the following lament of a girl roused from sleep in the cold wee hours:

Early in the night,
I dreamt of being married
— Oh, how kind my lover,
Oh how much we loved,
Clinging to each other!
Suddenly awakened,
My spirit in a tizzy,
I found my dream love gone!
Searching through my dreams,
I ordered that young man
By all means to await me
In my dreams to come.

Most of the best tea gardens lie in the more southerly part of eastern China, especially in the coastal provinces. As they are situated in mountainous areas where the climate is mild but misty, they are similar enough for one description to suffice. The following is an account of a visit paid to a garden in the Wu-I Mountains of Fukien in 1944.

In those days Fukien's north-south highway and the roads meandering from it were poorly surfaced and had dizzying curves, but the mountains, more forested than elsewhere in the country, were lovely enough to keep the traveller enthralled. At a small market township of one-storey buildings with the usual curling eaves but constructed of red brick instead of the grey brick favoured in other provinces, a smallish road branched off and wound its steep way into tea country. Presently the delicious scent of fresh young tea hung upon the breeze. The lorry I was riding in with a friend called Lin suddenly turned up a narrow track, passed under an archway inscribed with the garden's name and came to a halt amidst a complex of sheds where dozens of men were working busily.

In the sheds newly plucked leaves were being rolled, dried, partially fermented and then fired to convert them into oolong tea. The manager deputed a foreman to explain everything carefully; but having no interest in technical matters and eager to wander about the tea garden, I just nodded my head and looked wise until Lin and I were summoned to lunch in the office. Lunch was followed by some marvelous tea, and then, we were free to go.

To the left and right of the mountain path the land had been terraced, not with a series of flat terraces as for rice, but sloping ones planted with luxuriantly green tea bushes some three or four feet high, their scent intoxicating. As it was well after noon picking had stopped, but small groups of pickers were still to be seen. All were women, nearly all young. Like most peasants in that region, they wore high-collared jackets and baggy trousers of either blue or black cloth, but their garments were neat and spotlessly clean. The married women's hair looked as if it had been lacquered, being drawn up into a thick roll running back from above the forehead and protruding horizontally above the nape of the neck. In some cases a sort of top-

less cap covered just the front and sides of the hair. Their only ornaments were long silver hairpins topped with small pieces of smooth or carved green jade, and bangles of coarser jade. As for the young girls, their hair was worn in a thick, smooth plait which hung down behind or was wound round the head and bound with scarlet thread. Their ivory complexions were tinged with red as a result of exposure to the mountain winds, their dark eyes bright, their ready smiles delightfully unselfconscious.

Gazing at them appreciatively, Lin remarked: 'Good water here. You can tell from the clarity of their skin and the brightness of their eyes. Besides, good tea and water are generally found together. Here the springs bubble up and send their water tumbling over clear rocks and pebbles, as if trained by the old Tea Masters.'

'Lin,' I answered, my eyes still on some girls smiling back at us over their shoulders as they walked away, 'you come here a lot. Have you got to know some of them pretty well?'

'Can't be done,' he said. 'They are fond of fun and affectionate by nature, but accept no casual advances whether from city people or youths in their villages. It is the custom that betrothal must follow hard upon the lightest intimacy. What a pity! City girls with their lipsticks, powder and pencilled eyebrows cannot compare with these fresh-looking mountain girls. But then, of course, the water on the plains and in the valleys is different.'

Climbing higher, we came to a dilapidated temple that had stood there for centuries. The ridge, rising high above a curly roof with a double set of eaves, was ornamented in the local style with flamboyantly coloured and intricately patterned tracery, but the colours had softened with the years. Within, the flaking image of a deity presided over a crumbling altar on which stood a lighted oil lamp, a pair of tall red candles in heavy pewter holders and a pewter incense burner with gilded handles. The ash in the burner was stubbled with the thin red stems of burnt-out incense sticks. A flaking gilt table above the shrine proclaimed in huge black characters that we were in the holy presence of the mountain's guardian deity. Vertical tablets on either side promised blessings to those who behaved kindly to the people, animals and birds within his jurisdiction.

Adjoining the shrine hall were rooms: a kitchen and a bedroom for the use of the temple's solitary keeper, who was nowhere to be seen. The furnishings were sparse and crude, but we noticed an attractive tea set of good I-Hsing pottery, the teapot no larger than an orange, the cups scarcely bigger than thimbles. There could be no doubt that their owner was a tea man and one who knew how to prepare the kind of tea that is savoured like a liqueur brandy.

Behind the temple stood a well-like structure of ancient brick, fed by a pipe fashioned from sections of giant bamboo which carried water down from a spring higher up the mountain. We saw it cascading into the 'well', from which it overflowed into another bamboo pipe leading to a gully. A bamboo dipper hanging on a post invited passers-by to sample its clear, cold water.

The path continued to wind upwards. On the lower slopes of a cluster of pinnacles, the tea shrubs gave way to a forest of pines and then to some clumps of trees that included some belonging to a species I could not identify. 'These', said Lin in answer to my unspoken question, 'may or may not be wild, but they are descended from trees that grew here centuries ago—the tea trees we read about in old books. Notice how the peaks and the other trees growing around protect them from too much sunshine. Be sure the leaves are excellent. Probably the best tea in this garden comes from here.'

Looking at their leafy branches, I grew aware of a magical stillness. It was not silence, for the mountain wind sighed gustily and there were bird calls and small rustlings made by either birds or animals. It was peace. I began to feel that this was my true home, high above the world of dust from which I had risen. Lin must have felt this too, for he went off to sit on a flattish rock too far off for conversation to be necessary. For perhaps half an hour we sat there, gazing at trees and clouds, rapt in a state not far from bliss. But the afternoon grew chilly, so by common consent we rose to begin the downward climb.

Going down by a different route, we entered a secluded upland valley criss-crossed by streams shining in the late afternoon sunshine. Presently we stopped to rest at a small hamlet where, pressed against a wall of sheer rock, stood a rickety building surmounted by a tattered roof of thatch. Recognising it as a rural teahouse, we sat on a bench beside a rickety wooden table. From the nearest cottage a little girl ran out crying: 'The stove is alight. I shall bring you some tea, good not good?'

'Very good,' we answered with one voice, Lin adding, 'anything to go with it?'

The girl, who seemed to be about twelve or thirteen, nodded. 'Strangers mostly ask that,' she laughed. 'City people can't climb as much as three or four *li* without getting hungry. Grandma keeps a store of rice cakes just in case. They came here in a real tin! There's a dragon and a phoenix, one each side.'

She brought the tea. It was an oolong fit for Immortals, but served in bowls of rough, crudely glazed earthenware like a tea of no account. With it came a platter of sweet moon-shaped rice cakes so hard that I nearly cracked a tooth. Giggling at such ineptitude, the little Ah Mui explained that they needed dunking in the tea. Seeing her eye them longingly (they must have come from some market town and be, by her standards, unbelievably expensive), I told her to fetch a third bowl of tea and help herself to as many cakes as she liked. Her eyes grew round. Then she laughed. 'As many as I like? Oh, no, I must leave some for you.' As it turned out, she did eat all we left, then thanked us as gravely as if we had given her not just a few coppers but a golden hairpin. 'Goodbye, goodbye!' she cried as we walked away. 'Please forgive us for such a poor welcome.'

'There,' said Lin, as we strolled down through the valley, 'You see how these mountain girls are—illiterate yet good-mannered, full of fun yet dignified, and oh, how pretty! How I should like to live here, marry a simple, loyal girl ready to look after me properly and bear seven or eight children without the least fuss or bother. All this peace and quiet, the smell of tea buds, sparkling water, mountain food, up early in the morning when the birdsong grows clamorous, forest walks, kindly people, friendly animals unafraid of people, a neighbour or two who understand tea and chess, a cottage with some books and couple of stringed instruments. One could live like those scholars of old who, retiring before the age of thirty, entered the Way and became Immortals.'

'Hmm, yes,' I answered. 'After all, with the best of good tea always available one would not miss restaurants, shops, cinemas or whatever. But peace and quiet with seven or eight children?'

Lin smiled ruefully. 'You are right, but then, you see, with a very pretty wife and little else to do, that could hardly be avoided. There might be more than eight or nine.'

This picture of a Fukien tea garden as seen by a visitor is, of course, open to the charge of being overly idyllic. However, the cleanness and neatness of the tea girls we had met on our way up the mountain pointed to a standard of living superior to that of China's ubiquitous rice farmers. The days when tribute tea was harvested during a month of backbreaking labour had long vanished from memory. Though the pickers still had to work hard in early spring, when the best of a crop was harvested, during most of the year the lives of those permanently employed by the tea garden must have been pleasant enough, for they looked healthy and well fed; and one could see from their expressions that they were contented people. Later I learned that there are two kinds of picker: youngish girls, and middle-aged women from local villages whose fathers and husbands were almost certainly employed in the processing sheds; and others, mostly young girls with a sprinkling of even younger boys, who came from villages farther away to earn money with which to help support their parents or as a nest egg that would be useful after marriage. The latter tended to come seasonally (especially during spring) and were housed in dormitories belonging to the tea garden. While the wages of newcomers were likely to be small indeed, after receiving training pickers were well paid by the standards of those days.

The nature of the work required that they get up very early, but this was compensated for by their leaving off hours before the men working in the processing sheds. Like mountain-dwelling communities in many parts of the world, they had to provide their own amusements, which no doubt accounts for their being generally fond of—and good at—singing. Their songs were mainly love songs but had little to do with casual love, for the tea girls looked forward to making a 'good marriage,' by which they meant marrying into families where everyone, young or old, would be expected to work hard but might hope to make a joint income that would keep them all in moderate comfort. Indeed, the songs were sometimes a means to that end.

Tea songs are sung in chorus, the men and women singing alternate verses. Whereas opportunities for boys and girls to be alone together were rare or nonexistent, there was nothing to prevent individuals from expressing their feelings for each other with smiles and meaning looks while singing. When an understanding had been reached in this way, the boy could very likely persuade his elders to send matchmakers to talk things over with the girl's parents. The wording of the tea pickers' songs gave plenty of scope for this kind of understanding to arise, as will be seen from the lyric below:

BOY *Oh, little sister, neighbour dear,*
So famous for your pretty ways.
If only we could make a pair,
We'd be happy all our days.

Then, brother, ask my mum and dad.   GIRL
But as I've nothing, being poor,
To bring your folk and make them glad,
I'll feel ashamed if asked for more.

One scented hanky, don't you see,   BOY
Would make up for the things you lack.
Just give me one and they'll agree
To send betrothal presents back.

You whistle in the mountain air,   GIRL
While I stitch shoes with colours gay.
If those *are what you long to wear—*
Then, love play, love games every day!

    This song has a quaint simplicity like those of peasants in other lands; but its theme is typical of China, for it reflects the mores of a society where parents were the arbiters of marriage and where even the prettiest of girls might expect rejection if she lacked a sufficient trousseau. Therefore, love song though it is, only a few of the lines have a direct bearing on love, most of the others being concerned with parents and livelihood. The verse about shoes has a double meaning. Outwardly the girl seems to be saying, 'At least I have one or two useful skills to make up for my poverty,' but in fact in China shoes have esoteric implications and can be used in certain ways to symbolise a girl's love for a boy.

    In many parts of China there are rustic songs which speak of the special charms and warm-heartedness of tea girls. Their appeal has a direct connection with tea, for they owe their look of glowing health to the cool, fresh air and pure water which characterise the tea plant's natural habitat; and physical cleanliness is absolutely required of all workers in a tea garden. What is more, the lovely setting provided by woods, streams, rocks and the brilliant green of the tea plants must inevitably have an uplifting effect on the spirits of mountain-dwellers inhabiting a region too nearly akin to the subtropics for the winters to be long or rigorous.

Teahouses

In the days of the empire, aristocratic or scholarly tea votaries had special rooms or buildings rather like summerhouses to provide a perfect atmosphere for their tea sessions. The most splendid of their kind, still to be seen in some of Soochow's world-famed private gardens, were generally surrounded by a lotus pond or miniature lake and approached by a zigzag bridge. Square, circular or hexagonal in shape, they might have fantastic roofs with fancifully curling eaves supported on massive wooden pillars. If the walls were of brick there would be windows all around, perhaps differently shaped so as to resemble say, a fan, a bell, a flower, a leaf, a vase, a full moon and so on. Some had entire walls that could be folded back like the panels of movable screens; these, being made of translucent rice paper stretched across hinged wooden frames, could easily be folded or unfolded to suit the weather at any particular hour of the day or night. In cold weather the interior would be warmed by a charcoal brazier so one could sit snugly inside, gazing out across the water at the landscaped rocks and trees and admiring, say, massed chrysanthemums in autumn or moonlit snow in winter.

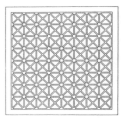

Private Teahouses

The furnishings were likely to be sparse: a couch, perhaps, and a small table with wooden chairs or porcelain stools, besides the essentials for practising the tea art in the traditional fashion, namely a water tub, a portable charcoal tea stove and shelves or a cupboard for the smaller accessories. These and the lanterns of painted horn or silken gauze hanging from the beams would invariably be elegant, never garish or ostentatious.

The pond, in addition to patches of massed lotus leaves, might have water irises and other flowers according to season, and curiously shaped rocks, perhaps brought from mountains over a thousand miles away, built up to form caves, grottoes, tiny waterfalls or miniature cataracts. The surrounding garden would have no lawns or flowerbeds but be laid out to form a varied landscape with tiny hills, willow clumps, bamboo groves, contorted pines or trees notable for springtime blossom or autumn tints. Everything in sight would combine to engender the poetic feeling associated with tea drinking.

Besides tea sessions, such pavilions were used for various scholarly pursuits: playing ancient tunes upon a silk-stringed lute whose melody was scarcely louder than the hum of a bumble bee; having a game of chess with one hundred and sixty black or white stone pieces for each player; improvising poems in honour of flowers of the season, autumn moonlight, sunset clouds; burning rare incense, guessing poetic riddles, intoning notable poems or essays ranging back for over two thousand years. Nothing coarse must be allowed to intrude, and even flowers and incense should be banished before a tea session lest their heavy fragrance mar the subtle aroma of fine tea.

Another and much commoner kind of private teahouse typified the ancient ideal of frugal simplicity. Its light thatched roof would be supported on thin, unlacquered wooden or bamboo poles, its walls constructed of papered latticework. The furniture it contained would be rustic in character, made of plain wood, bamboo, rattan, gnarled tree roots and the like. Everything would have its natural colour—the white of rice paper, the yellows of straw and bamboo, the various browns of unpainted wood. Often there would be a pond, but the surrounding landscape should be faithful to untamed nature or else include such rural scenes as orchards, vegetable patches, rice fields. To suit this background, earthenware tea-things would be preferred to those of fine porcelain—although white or blue porcelain cups would be acceptable.

In households with little land to spare for such a purpose, a small tearoom often stood in the courtyard immediately adjacent to the master's study.* In Europe and America I have seen summerhouses that cried out to be transformed into teahouses and seemed as if built for that very purpose, so they would require little adaptation to conform with the rules set forth in that chapter, which state that there

*There is a description of one in Chapter 3.

should be a space nearby but conveniently out of sight where certain large or unsightly objects can be stored so as to avoid clutter (though these days such objects are scarcely necessary, thanks to tap water and electric kettles). By having rather sparse appointments one can make a small room look more spacious than it is. As for the summerhouse's surroundings, it may not be practicable or necessary to alter these much, but if possible there should be several of the following within view: water of some sort (a stream or pond, or a miniature cascade made with the help of a few rocks and a hidden tap); trees (especially pine, cedar or flowering trees); distant hills and/or nearby rocks. Also, there should be some means of boiling water without having to fetch a kettleful from the kitchen, for the enjoyment of tea is enhanced by the pleasant sounds of bubbling water and hissing steam. A small portable stove fed with smokeless charcoal is naturally ideal, but an electric ring is acceptable because it is clean and odourless. Using a gas stove can impair the aroma of very fine teas, but of course one generally has to make do with whatever happens to be in the house. There are no hard and fast rules.

Public Teahouses

HISTORY

Before the Communist Revolution every Chinese city had innumerable teahouses, and they were also common in rural areas boasting scenic spots, ancient temples, famous springs or tea gardens. The role they played in people's lives was unique. From dawn to almost midnight young and old frequented them: some to quench thirst and hunger or merely to relax; others to sample various kinds of tea but also to talk business, make deals, seal bargains, arrange marriages, see friends, entertain visitors or local luminaries, exchange ideas, discuss everything under the sun, spout poetry, listen to storytellers, strike up acquaintanceships, get warm in winter or cool down in summer, observe regional customs when travelling, drown worries, arbitrate disputes, give pet birds an airing—the list is endless. People might drop in for a quick bowl of tea between two engagements, or idle away the entire day there for the price of a few bowls of tea and a snack or two.

As far back as the T'ang dynasty there were public teahouses, but they seem to have catered chiefly to connoisseurs of fine tea. During the Ming period that trend seems not to have altered greatly, for the walls of tearooms were sometimes adorned with the works of famous painters and calligraphers, an indication that their patrons were wealthy and cultured. However, by Ch'ing times urban teahouses had become much like those I visited in the 1930s: in other words, there were various kinds that catered jointly to almost all segments of the population, ranging from the well-to-do to apprentices, artisans, workmen, river boatmen, rickshaw pullers and villagers come to town to sell their produce.

As a traveller I was interested to note how these teahouses varied from province to province, reflecting differences in lifestyle due to climate, topography, cultural and social mores. Travelling, mostly alone, across China's mountains and rivers, I enjoyed making friends with teahouse people in each locality. In their genial atmosphere it was easy to chat with staff and customers, the more so as, in many provinces, customers were accommodated at large tables with long benches where they sat cheek by jowl with whoever happened to be there. Most people seemed delighted to chat with a visitor coming from the outer rim of the 'four seas'.

North China

In the north, people drank tea many, many times a day, but only two broad categories of tea were really popular, namely green tea and flower tea. However, in large cities such as Peking and the nearby port of Tientsin one could find various teas brought from all over China. Tientsin, at that time a more 'Westernised' city than the old capital, had a number of so-called 'tea gardens', but this was a misnomer for most were located in multi-storey buildings among tiers of shops and entertainment places ranged around a central courtyard. They were in fact scarcely tea places at all, for one had to buy an admission ticket to what usually proved to be a vaudeville performance with the audience sitting at tables eating titbits and drinking wine or tea while watching acrobats, swordsmen, dancers and drum-girl storytellers perform in turn. If there was standing room only, a latecomer would scarcely hope for so much as a single cup of tea.

What I liked in Tientsin were the tea stores, their walls lined with hundreds of wooden drawers each with the name of a tea carved on it in green calligraphy. Some names were fanciful, others poetic or with historical associations, and yet others were geographic,—but all were beautiful. Better still, there would be piles of jasmine buds filling the store with their fragrance. What the northern Chinese call flower tea is generally middle or inferior quality green or 'red' tea steeped with two or three fresh buds, not processed with dried flowers as in the south. Fine teas were never mixed with flowers as the delicate flavours would be swamped by their penetrating scent.

Peking used to have hundreds of teahouses. Alas, on a recent visit (in 1982) I saw none! The new regime, having pulled down the greater part of the old city consisting mainly of beautiful Chinese-style houses built around tree-filled courtyards, had replaced the demolished buildings with 'Stalinesque' apartment blocks of uniform drabness. In the old days everyone, unless desperately poor, drank quantities of tea. Rising early as was their custom, patrons began filling the teahouses soon after dawn; others took tea at home or at their places of work. In homes, the first tea of the day would be served ceremoniously to the grandparents; in shops, to the owners or manager; then to the rest of the family or apprentices in order of seniority.

This done, everyone relaxed and drank tea when they felt like it. Friends meeting before noon would seldom say 'Good morning', but 'Have you had tea yet?'

There were Peking teahouses that dispensed nothing but tea, apart from saucers of salted melon seeds or peanuts to stimulate thirst; others served light snacks. In those with more than one storey, customers who went upstairs (where one paid a few more cents for a pot of tea) would be regaled in the evenings by a relay of drum girls, pretty female storytellers who sang old stories in piercingly high voices while prancing around dramatically and marking the rhythm with hand drum and clappers. Meanwhile, an old woman swaying on 'golden lilies' (tiny bound feet) went from table to table carrying a huge fan inscribed on one side with the names of stories the girls could sing and on the other with the names of the singers, in case a customer desired to make a girl's closer acquaintance rather than merely listen to her graphic recital. Even so, the main function of teashops, the selling of freshly brewed tea, was never lost sight of so the atmosphere in no way reminded me of those detestable Tientsin 'tea gardens'. In those days Peking, having recently been the seat of so glorious a being as the Son of Heaven, still valued old-world courtesy, elegance and charm. Teashop attendants and customers were mostly friendly and courteous and the same was true of almost everybody. Whenever I dropped into a curio shop or a store selling expensive things such as silk or brocades I would be bowed in by blue-robed apprentices with cries of welcome, then served with good tea and imported cigarettes, and later bowed out (whether I had bought anything or not) with the gracious injunction 'Please condescend to visit us again.'

The magnificent parks, including former palace gardens, were dotted with tea places offering views of multicoloured roofs, lacquered galleries and pavilions standing amidst centuries-old pines and cedars. Here and there were porcelain tubs containing goldfish,

of which there were said to be over a hundred varieties. Other tea places looked out on banks of peonies or fruit trees bowed beneath a weight of blossom, foliage or snow according to the season.

An especially famous teahouse was the tall Green Cloud Pavilion, which stood in the grounds of the Temple of Kuan-Yin. Its elegance recalled the days of imperial princes and scholar-statesmen, and its choicest teas appropriately included Iron Goddess of Mercy (*T'ieh-Kuan-Yin*) tea brought all the way from Fukien's Wu-I Mountains. It was a special treat to drink this admirable tea in the lavishly appointed top storey, which bore the curious name of Jade Teapot Springtime.

In contrast to such aristocratic elegance, teahouses in the pleasure quarter of the city, known as the Heavenly Bridge, usually provided drum-girl story performances, conjuring or acrobatic shows. Here one could choose from among more ordinary teas or bring along a packet of one's own and just pay the cost of infusion. The general favourite was a cheap but unusual tea called notable remnants, a blend of rejected 'sweepings' from many kinds of expensive tea.

The South-East

Not only do the finest teas come from the south-east provinces of Kiangsu, Chekiang and Fukien, but the most attractive teahouses were (and perhaps still are) to be found there, for scenic mountain springs and tea gardens abound. Moreover, Kiangsu and Chekiang had come to surpass the north in culture long ago, under Sung, Ming and Ch'ing, whereas North China (with the exception of Peking) had declined on account of inroads made by alien tribes from beyond the Great Wall which had intermittently set up independent dynasties in the Yellow River region; indeed, they twice subdued the whole country, giving birth to the Yüan (Mongol) and Ch'ing (Manchu) dynasties.

Having never visited a teahouse in Nanking, Chiang Kai-shek's capital throughout the greater part of the 1930s, I shall paraphrase an amusing account of the situation there in those days by my tea brother, Yü-Yü. According to him, Nanking teahouses, whether they served just tea or tea and snacks, offered rather indifferent tea. There were also hundreds of little shops open day and night, each of which housed a so-called tea stove but served only water—boiling, warm or cold! Busy all day long, they were packed out in the hour following dawn. If someone wanted tea he would have to bring his own tea leaves and a teapot, fill it himself at the stove, throw down a copper and hurry away to make room for the queue of people patiently awaiting their turn. These places were in great demand: housewives unable or too lazy to light a fire at home could bring any size of utensil and for a single copper buy water for tea, for washing their faces or feet, or for any other purpose. Outside the door a host of city folk and peasants come in from the country could be seen squatting on their haunches washing, shaving or else drinking tea made with leaves they had brought with them. Obviously, these tealess 'tea stoves' served a widespread public need!

Memorable teahouses were to be found in such ancient cities as Yangchow, Soochow and Hangchow, which were famous for their culture and the beauty of their womenfolk. Teahouses in Yangchow and Soochow were tastefully appointed single- or two-storey buildings, often standing in a garden. Yangchow overlooks a lake, while Soochow has a maze of picturesque waterways; and both had teahouses overlooking a panorama of richly decorated pleasure boats gliding past banks lined with bamboo clumps and willow trees. For the price of a pot of tea one could spend hours enjoying the watery scenery and cooling breezes. For patrons who found this poetic pastime too tame there were separate rooms with singers and storytellers.

Hangchow, another lakeside city, had some of the best teahouses in China, the pale green teas served there being picked locally and therefore deliciously fresh. Along the paths leading from the city to springs, temples and notable scenic spots, rustic teahouses stood in rows. Those on the mountain side had for centuries been the property of Buddhist monks—a feature seldom found elsewhere. In early spring, crowds of tea votaries came to watch tea girls singing at their work on the mountainside. Not far from the city is Tiger-Run Spring, which stands in the grounds of a monastery dating back to T'ang times. Its water is held to be the perfect mate for the superb Lung-Ching (Dragon's Well) tea that grows nearby. To taste a cup of Lung-Ching made with Tiger-Run water is a Chinese tea man's fondest dream. In the words of my Tea Brother: 'Fortunate indeed are those tea people who have a chance to visit Hangchow!'

Some Central Provinces

Hundreds of miles to the south-west of Hangchow lies Kiangsu Province, noted for its Ching-Tê clay pits and the exquisite porcelain teacups that, ideally speaking, should go with I-Hsing teapots. This apart, Kiangsu was for more than a millenium the seat of the Heavenly Master who dwelt on Dragon-and-Tiger Mountain, whence the last to bear that title fled to Taiwan before the advance of the Red Army. The Taoist recluses dwelling in the neighbouring mountains were fond of tea but often short of money. When they dropped in at teahouses they would earn a little by singing Taoist songs and beating hand drums made of a hollowed-out segment of giant bamboo with pigskin stretched over the ends. Of their songs, which had a characteristically Taoist flavour, there was one which ran:

sometimes called the 'Taoist Pope'

An elderly priest in an age-old temple
Himself tends the incense, himself beats the drum.
The offerings he makes are of coarse mountain viands.
The yellow sun sinks midst a tangle of pines;

Autumn stars shine through gaps in the wall.
Why bother to lock the tumble-down gate?
Now it's pitch dark within. Quietly he sits
On a tattered rush mat, mind in Samādhi,
Then brews midnight tea by the stove's ruddy light.

A more sophisticated Taoist song heard by Chang T'ieh-Chün in a Kiangsu teahouse brings together the tea art's three prime essentials—fine tea, pure water and beautiful ceramics.

I had sipped some tea
*From a 'rabbit-fur' chien,**
An exquisite fragrance
Clung to my palate.
True, a kettle of snow
Would have added some charm,
But the height of refinement
Depends on the potter.

*'Rabbit-fur' is the name of a design anciently used for tea utensils.

Several writers have noted how wonderfully the singing of the 'Cloud-Wanderers' evoked an atmosphere beautifully appropriate to the spirit of tea.

Bordering the western part of Kiangsu is Hunan Province, where everything pertaining to food and drink was astonishingly large—heavy tables, sturdy benches, outsize rice bowls and chopsticks so long that one might think they were to be used for putting food into the mouths of those sitting opposite rather than one's own! Inevitably, tea came in enormous bowls; yet the locals would drink off several bowlfuls in quick succession.

On the sacred mountain of Nan Yeo in that province I spent some nights in a Taoist monastery near the path winding to the peak. Outside the gate was a tea shanty, placed there for the convenience of thirsty pilgrims. As the recluses served good tea in the refectory it did not occur to me to patronise the shanty until I happened to notice that the big tea bowls set before travellers contained a strange reddish liquid with solid-looking objects floating near the surface. This, I now learn was a Hunanese delicacy. The tea leaves had been boiled with 'five-flavour beans', that is, beans flavoured with sweet, sour, bitter, pungent and salty ingredients! Though its taste was unpalatable to me, politeness demanded that I swallow down two bowlfuls. Still, the experience was of interest because it gave me an idea of how the commoner kinds of tea had tasted in T'ang times, when all sorts of ingredients were boiled in the water to be used for infusing tea.

The province of Kweichow adjoins the western border of Hunan. As it happened, I arrived there in company with the Oxford Regius Professor of Greek. We had been invited to visit a university which, having recently been evacuated from a maritime province invaded by the Japanese, was almost destitute of books and laboratory equipment. Lest we be disappointed, our hosts put on a sumptuous luncheon, pressing us to drink cup after cup of the fiery *maotai* spirit distilled in that locality. Hours later when we had said goodbye, heads still swimming, I took the professor to a teahouse, explaining that several bowls of strong Chinese tea would banish the fumes of alcohol. Being far from sober, I did not give a thought to the characteristics of the only Kweichow teahouse I entered before leaving for a neighbouring province. However, tea-book author Chang T'ieh-Chün, himself a native of that province, writes of its teahouses affectionately. Recalling the saying that in Kweichow 'fine weather never lasts three days; level ground never extends a mile', he explains that the local people were too poor to loiter all day in teahouses, which seldom filled up much before sunset. Tea was infused in small, lidded bowls from which one drank while nibbling such oddments as salted mallow seeds or salted popcorn. The atmosphere was extremely friendly: children were seldom charged for a bowl of tea when they dropped in to listen to the storytellers.

This huge 'Province of Four Rivers' sprawls over a large part of West China and used to function as a virtually independent state during troublous times; in the past it was not easy to approach except by sailing up the Yangtze River. For both these reasons it had more than a fair share of tyrannous local officials and consequently of secret societies, smugglers, vagabonds and river pirates—a state of affairs mirrored by the colourful clientele of its teahouses. An old saying, 'In the Yangtze there is water; on Mêng-Shan Peak there's tea', is a reminder that the province has both good tea and good water, which is why it has attracted tea men throughout the ages.

Some of the teahouses were big enough to accommodate several hundred patrons at thirty or forty long tables with benches on either side. Besides merchants, shopkeepers, artisans and other harmless people, the customers included a fair sprinkling of smugglers, black marketeers and members of secret societies. Perhaps it was for self-protection that they recruited their young attendants from among the junior ranks of the secret societies. These genial youths were extraordinarily deft at their job, but they liked to use thieves' slang and double talk or to sing out witty couplets in response to orders. Though dressed in drab cotton clothes, they were young men of talent. To down-at-heels, thirsty-looking customers embarrassed when confronted by the reckoning, the boys might sing: 'For this across-the-river tea you do not have to pay a fee,' or 'We'll chalk it up on the billowy waves.' An unusually liberal tip might elicit a chorus of: 'Peach blossom in summer! Tha-a-a-ank you!'

Their deftness lay partly in bringing the tea leaves you favoured or a refill of tobacco for your water pipe almost before you had finished giving the order, partly out of sheer dexterity. A lad carrying a fabulously large kettle would glide through the crowds and cascade the boiling water into your bowl, never spilling a drop even if he poured it from on high over the heads and shoulders of half a dozen people! Orders for snacks would be shouted across the room in fanciful couplets unintelligible to newcomers, but when the food arrived it would be right to the last detail: 'A bowl of boiled chicken noodles with extra chili but no parsley,' or whatever.

The entertainment offered sometimes included stories chanted by groups of little girls thumping pigskin and bamboo drums hung with strings of coins that emitted a gay tintinnabulation. However good the service and entertainment, the tea was choice, the price modest.

The Far South

Cantonese-style teahouses long ago spread to Hong Kong and have since exercised a world-wide influence. In most countries there are now Chinese restaurants which dispense tea and teahouse-style snacks (*dimsum*) at lunch time.

Traditionally, tea and *dimsum* were served for breakfast. Rising early, the Cantonese would fling on their clothes and make a beeline for the nearest teahouse. When I was there the city of Canton must have had some thousands of these establishments, their several storeys furnished with polished blackwood furniture inset with beautifully grained Ta-Li marble. As the prices increased storey by storey, the top floor drew the wealthier patrons. The owners of pet birds usually arrived about an hour after dawn, cage in hand; for it was the custom to take birds out for an airing in the hour when *ch'i* (life force) is at its purest. Tea, of which there would be at least six kinds to choose from, was infused in lidded bowls (*chung*) from which one poured it into small handleless cups.

The snacks in those days were brought round by boys, clad in undervests and drawers, on trays suspended from their necks. (The present-day use of trolley-wheeling glamour girls had not come into vogue.) One breakfasted at a teahouse to drink tea and sample a range of titbits that changed from day to day—not to gaze at pretty girls. *Dimsum* were commonly available from six in the morning until noon: hours when romantic feelings tend not to be obtrusive. From the end of lunchtime onwards only tea and sweets were served; but in the evenings there might be musicians and singers, including glamorous ladies in high-collared, ankle-length gowns, for it is then that tea drinking and romance may go hand in hand.

The sedate customers in the upper rooms, clad in long silk gowns, would fan themselves and sip tea with smiling decorum; whereas in the room nearer street level most would be wearing proletarian jackets and trousers of black silk gauze specially treated so as to be cool but not transparent. Untroubled by decorum, they might draw both feet up to the chair seat and stay perched there with their knees at chin level. Though the Chinese have been using chairs for the last twelve hundred years, postures adopted by the Cantonese lower orders seemed to reflect a hankering for the floor cushions used in ancient times.

Cantonese teahouses did a roaring trade. As the attendants had no time to walk over to the cashier's desk, bills were dispensed with; when a party rose to go, a waiter would tot up the number of empty bowls and snack saucers on the table, make a quick calculation and shout the reckoning to the cashier, using a special teahouse code, saying for instance, '*One* wee-ee-eek', meaning seven cents, 'Eight horor-orses', meaning eight cents.

Cantonese snacks are probably the most delicious titbits ever devised, but unfortunately the Cantonese are so dedicated to the pleasures of eating that the quality of the tea they drink is less worthy of attention. To this day in Hong Kong there are diners who gulp down whole glassfuls of expensive French brandy, drinking 'bottoms up' each time, as though resenting the interruption to their eating. The contemplative mood in which one sips fine tea is not for such as these!

During a recent trip to Canton, which since my last visit had experienced several decades of Communist government, I saw not a single teahouse; if there are some they must be few and far between. In less than thirty-five years the lifestyle of the Chinese people, preserved for century upon century, has changed beyond recognition. No doubt some former abuses have been uprooted, but it is saddening to see how drab daily life has become. In the old days the best teas were naturally beyond a lot of people's means, but visiting ordinary teahouses was comfortably within the means of even very poor people. That such places are now rare and in many places nonexistent indicates official disapproval of unproductive leisure, but now that the Chinese Government has begun revising some of its earlier policies there is a chance that teahouses will once again become a feature of urban life.

A recent article in the *Washington Post* relates that the Red Lantern teahouse in Chengtu, capital of Szechuan Province, is once again providing its customers with storytelling in the traditional fashion. For an admission price of seven cents customers get a bowl of jasmine tea and are entertained with dramatic stories relating to the dynasties of long ago. The seventy-year-old professional storyteller, now back in business after a decade during which storytellers were persecuted for 'propagating feudalism', has a repertoire to be proud of. Having memorised the better part of ten different epics, he is well acquainted with literally hundreds of stories, for each epic occupies three months when delivered at the rate of two hours per evening. He tells them with gusto, mimicking the voices of men and women, high and low, young and old, with vigorous miming and a wide range of facial expressions. That such teahouses are permitted to flourish again augurs well for the happiness and welfare of the many.

Ten Thousand Teas

'Ten thousand' in Chinese signifies a large, unspecifiable number. No one has ever listed all the teas in China, past and present, for even in modern times the names of new teas are arrived at unsystematically in accordance with all kinds of factors, such as times of harvesting, natural shape and colour of the leaves, colour and appearance after processing, place of origin, poetic fancy, legendary or historical references, marketing effectiveness, personal whim and so on.

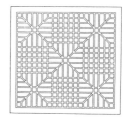

Of the Chinese teas becoming more widely available outside China today, almost all fall into one of the following categories: *green* (unfermented); *oolong* (semi-fermented); *red* (fully fermented and called 'black' tea in English); *white* which is rare these days except for certain kinds of P'u-Êrh tea or some inferior teas made to look white during processing; and, in some parts of the world, *brick* tea (usually fashioned from red tea, but sometimes from one of the others). Flower teas can be processed from any of the above categories, so they are not included in this list. Whether the quality of tea is good, bad or indifferent depends on many factors but particu-

see page 86

larly on the nature and locality of the bushes or trees from which it is culled. The categories listed above, however, all relate to processing, as theoretically all of them can be produced from any kind of fresh tea leaf.

Occasionally the name of a tea is sufficient indication of the general category it belongs to: for instance, Dragon's Well is invariably green and Iron Goddess of Mercy always denotes a partly fermented tea, just as Ch'i-Mên (keemun) is surely a 'red' (black) tea. However, most tea names give no indication as to whether the processed form is green or semi-fermented. All those mentioned in this book, unless specifically described as red (black) teas, are either semi-fermented or green. People accustomed only to black teas will do an injustice to the green and semi-fermented varieties—and probably find them unpalatable—if they adulterate them with milk, lemon, sugar or whatever.

As with many good things in this life, a taste for really fine teas has to be cultivated. If a person finds a famous tea disappointing to begin with, he or she should reflect that lovers of wine, beer, cheese, tobacco and so on rarely liked them on first acquaintance or knew how to distinguish those of high quality from the others.

In some cases a tea name is preceded by a few words which indicate the time of harvesting. This is a very important matter, for the finest grades of leaf are harvested before the Clear Light Festival, which falls late in March or early in April, so the leaves are tiny and marvellously fragrant. The next finest are plucked between that festival and the onset of the spring rains, while the leaves are still small and tender. Therefore tea votaries who can afford to buy the best are not satisfied by a very good name such as Dragon's Well. They look at the Chinese characters printed just before the name to see if the leaves were harvested 'before the light' or at least 'before the rains', whereas purchasers who require cheaper varieties of a famous tea are satisfied with those labelled 'after the rains', which indicates that the leaves will be larger and less tender. Unfortunately many of the high-class teas marketed today do not have the time of harvesting marked on their packaging, so until the purchaser has gained experience the only thing to do is to judge by the price range of several teas bearing the name of the desired brand.

Another way of classifying teas is according to their texture after processing. The categories are as follows:

LOOSE-LEAF TEA

By far the commonest category in modern times. It is divided into five subcategories:
1. *small leaf* (usually excellent, but not invariably so)
2. *broken leaf* (ranging from excellent to poor)
3. *large leaf* (which may be good but seldom excellent)
4. *fannings*
5. *dust*

No knowledgeable tea drinker would give any consideration at all to the last two. As for tea bags, there is nothing inherently wrong with them *per se*, but the fact is that many of them contain fannings or dust, which are the poorest and cheapest form of loose-leaf tea. Personally, I refuse to use tea bags unless positively assured that they contain no fannings or dust—these being what might be called the dross accumulated during processing.

TEA PASTE

Archaic and now rarely to be seen these days, except for a medicinal form of P'u-Êrh tea.

POWDERED TEA

Archaic, but still used in Japan for the tea ceremony.

CAKED TEA

Made from dried tea paste. The commonest form in ancient times but seldom seen today, except in the form known as brick tea.

BRICK TEA

Oblong blocks of tightly compressed tea leaves, usually red (black). They are still popular in Central Asia, Russia and certain other countries, but are rarely to be seen in Europe or America.

A modern tea brick (wholly consisting of compressed tea).

Lung-Ching (Dragon's Well)

Many Chinese connoisseurs affirm that the top grades of this delicately flavoured green tea can nowhere in the world be surpassed for colour, aroma and flavour. Produced in Chekiang Province near Hangchow's beautiful West Lake, it grows on several peaks of the T'ieh Mu mountain range. It is now increasingly on sale in Chinese shops in China, Europe and America, but the finest qualities are expensive and may be hard to come by outside China and Hong Kong. They are plucked before the Clear Light Festival or at least before the spring rains have fallen. The very choicest come from a part of the mountain called Lion's Peak, where picking takes place before each tender sprout has more than a single leaf. Their fragrance is so delicate that the leaves must be skilfully packaged or kept in completely airtight tea caddies: exposure to the air would quickly ruin the flavour and aroma. Moreover, green and semi-green tea should be brewed by steeping the leaves in water several degrees below boiling point and using spotless utensils guarded from all contact with kitchen or other sources of extraneous odours. Overlong steeping will make the infusion bitter; if insufficiently steeped, it will taste insipid.

Around the year AD 250, so runs the story, a Taoist affirmed that there must be a dragon lurking in a certain spring not far from Hangchow. Having made this discovery at a time when the farmers had long been praying for rain, he implored the well dragon to come to their rescue. Instantly, clouds came rushing in from every side and poured forth timely rain. On this account the name of an old temple adjoining the spring is known as Dragon's Well Monastery, and the tea derives its name from the same legend.

Another source relates that a poor widow living in that particular vicinity owned a few tea trees and used their produce to brew tea for peasants harvesting tea nearby. One day a rich merchant, hearing of her kindness, remarked, 'A good-hearted woman like you deserves to be wealthy'. 'I am lucky not to starve,' she answered, smiling. Glancing round, he noticed a large stone mortar which happened to be full of leaves deposited by neighbouring tea trees over the years. 'Want to sell that old mortar?' he asked. 'If so, I'll come back and cart it off tomorrow.' She took the money offered, so the next morning he came back with some workmen to cart it away. To his surprise, the shabby old mortar had been swept and scoured. 'You can see I've made it nice for you,' smiled the old woman. 'All those leaves came in handy to manure my tea trees.' Heaven had clearly rewarded her charitableness by endowing the leaf mould with miraculous properties, for not long afterwards her eighteen tea trees put forth jade-green leaves the like of which had never before been seen. Such, according to this alternative account, was the origin of Dragon's Well tea. It is said that the old woman prospered greatly.

Those well acquainted with this kind of tea affirm that it achieves the utmost perfection when prepared with clear water from Tiger-Run Spring, which 'miraculously' appeared close to a temple not far from the tea garden. During the reign of the T'ang Emperor Yüan Ho (806-821) there was another terrible drought, and once again the people of Hangchow prayed vainly to the gods for rain. One day Abbot Hsing K'ung saw two tigers rush out from the nearby forest and start running to and fro in the temple grounds. Suddenly water began bubbling up from the ground trodden by their feet. From that day to this the spring has never run dry. Its water is marvellously clear, and when used to brew Dragon's Well tea the infusion looks like liquid jade besides giving forth a delicious fragrance that lingers on the palate. As a Ming visitor remarked centuries later: 'I'd love to be a monk living here always with *such* tea and *such* water for companions!'

The tea gardens in that vicinity have a white sandy soil, and the climate is ideal for growing tea. Indeed, all the tea thereabouts is of excellent quality. The other local teas are so similar to Dragon's Well in flavour and appearance that even experts are hard put to it to detect differences. However, it is said that the finest Dragon's Well leaves, which grow on Lion's Peak, on being infused cause the water to turn an orange colour for a minute or two before it changes to jade-green, a green which no matter how much time elapses does not become muddy-looking or yellowish.

In these days when so many of China's teahouses have apparently disappeared, it is good to know that the one adjacent to Tiger-Run Spring still thrives and that visitors are regaled there with high-quality Dragon's Well tea brewed with that peerless water.

Other Green Teas

Of the many green teas, the following are especially notable:

Shih-Fêng (Lion's Peak)   These are in fact varieties of Dragon's Well or closely similar to it.

Pai-Yün (White Cloud)

Pao-Yün (Jewelled Cloud)

Shou-Mei (Old Man's Eyebrows)   This tea has been sun-dried and subjected to a minimum of processing, so its colour and aroma are as close as possible to those of fresh leaves.

Tz'ê-Sun (Purple Sprout)

Hsieh-Tou (Snow Gorge)

Jin-Chu (Sun-Poured, also known as Sun-Fused)

The last named was so highly prized in days gone by that it received honourable mention in many a tea book. It is produced on sun-fused peaks in the district of Shao-Hsing, where the weather is sunnier than in most tea-growing areas so the flavour of the tea is unusual, sun-loving tea plants being rare. The leaves are long, white and slender, the infusion sweet and full-bodied. Already popular in Sung times, towards the end of the Ming dynasty it became known as *Lan-Hsüeh* (Orchid Snow)—whereby hangs a tale.

The scholar Chang Yo, to whom it owes that picturesque name, was a Ming official who sadly witnessed the overthrow of that dynasty by the Manchus, so though he lived to be eighty-eight the latter part of his life was passed in enforced retirement made bearable by his love for books and tea. Before the change of dynasty in the year 1638, when he had reached the age of forty-two, he visited Nanking, where lived a seventy-year-old Tea Master called Min Wên-Shui. Longing to taste a brew prepared by the master's hands, he rushed off to call on the old gentleman. Min happened to be out, so Chang decided to wait for him. Presently the Master entered the gate, but before Chang could introduce himself, exclaimed: 'Ah, I forgot my walking stick! Kindly sit down while I retrieve it.' Poor Chang Yo, left seated on a cold bench in the outer courtyard, had a long and weary wait. When at last the old man returned, though obviously surprised to find his visitor still there, he courteously enquired the reason for his visit. 'Sir,' replied Chang Yo fervently, 'I have long heard of you with admiration. So great is my longing to taste your tea that I vow not to leave this spot without having done so!' Touched by such single-mindedness, Master Min immediately led him to a room where some tea-things were standing ready. They included a Ching-Ch'i earthenware pot and a spotlessly clean Ch'eng-Hua tea bottle.*

Having prepared the stove, the host made tea in a manner that won Chang Yo's deepest respect, for later he said of it: 'With the speed of wind and rain, it flowed into the bowls, its fragrance overwhelming.' When Min told him, tongue in cheek, that it had been made with

*The ancient form of teakettle.

Han-Yüan leaf, his guest begged to differ and correctly guessed its real name. Much impressed, the old man next remarked that the water had been brought all the way from Mount Hui, at which Chang cried: 'If that were so, how could it possibly be so fresh?' However, this time the master stuck by his assertion, explaining that before drawing the water he had thoroughly cleansed the spring and waited for it to refill. Moreover, the water had been transported in stone containers.

Delighted to have such an appreciative guest, Min presently brewed a second pot, whereupon Chang, lifting his bowl and inhaling the fragrance, remarked: 'I believe, sir, that the tea you served earlier had been picked in autumn, whereas this one is made with leaves plucked in spring.' Master Min was by now smiling broadly. 'Young man, you are remarkable,' he said. 'Though I have lived seventy years and met many, many tea lovers, I know of none so perceptive as yourself. It would be an honour to have you as a friend.' Min was so famous in the world of tea that the privilege of tasting tea made by his hands was not easily attained. As to being accepted as his tea friend, this was striking testimony to the younger man's talents.

Some Green Teas from Szechuan Province

This huge province in West China consists of vast, well-watered, fertile plains surrounded by hills and mountains of which many are densely forested. The tea gardens on their slopes have long been famous in Chinese history; but in modern times, though popular locally, Szechuan teas are less widely known than they used to be to the natives of other provinces. However, two of them, Green City and Hidden Peak, are the subjects of old poems and legends beloved of tea men.

CH'ING-CH'ÊNG (GREEN CITY) This tea is also known by the strange name of Chang-Jên, (Wife's Father). Green City Mountain, so called because of its fancied resemblance to a walled city, is a lovely place where, while staying in a

Taoist hermitage, I had the local tea served to me by the spiritual descendants of a line of Taoists going back to very ancient times. Their old-world charm and graceful gestures won my heart; so though I drank their tea with the greatest pleasure I do not remember much about the flavour. In any case, the following story about it testifies to its excellence.

During the period of the T'ang dynasty Hsüan Tsung, the 'Bright Emperor', once fled to Szechuan during a rebellion led by his one-time trusted favourite, An Lu-Shan. While travelling through that province he dreamt of a famous Taoist Master, the Venerable Sun Szê-Mo, whose death had been recorded a century earlier. In the dream, Master Sun descended Green City Mountain to ask His Majesty to procure some flowers of sulphur he required for an experiment. Accordingly, the emperor graciously ordered that ten catties of this substance be dispatched to the mountain. On its lower slopes the imperial messenger encountered a very old Taoist with a flowing beard, white eyebrows and brilliant eyes, who said: 'Put the sulphur on that great rock over there. You will find a message of thanks carved on its surface. Please copy it with your writing brush and show the words to the Lord of Ten Thousand Years.' No sooner had the official done so than both the rock and the old Taoist suddenly vanished. The Emperor, however, received the message and, on his return to the capital, a rumour spread that Master Sun, now more than two hundred years old, was still living on that mountain!

The truth of this rumour received apparent confirmation from what happened to a Buddhist monk who lived in Chengtu, the provincial capital. One day he received a message asking him to hurry to Green City Mountain and chant a holy text to a sick old man. Following the messenger, he arrived at a lonely hut built of bamboo and reeds. There he was ceremoniously welcomed by a ragged old man leaning on a pear-wood staff, whose long earlobes almost reached his shoulders. His hair was disordered; his eyes shone with a strange brilliance. While the monk was chanting, the ancient knelt in front of him. Then the servant produced a vegetarian meal as plain as could be but tasting like ambrosia. This was followed by some orange-coloured tea, made with long and slender leaves, that emitted a 'fragrant cloud of steam'. As he sipped this rare beverage, the monk felt as though 'caressed by a spring wind'. Eagerly he asked its name, to be informed by his host: 'It's just a local tea. How could one compare it with the good tea you people buy in the city?' 'Why, it's the best I have ever tasted,' replied the monk. 'It's positively a fairy tea. I never thought to find anything like it in this lonely place.' Later, as the servant was escorting him down the mountain, the monk impulsively inquired as to his master's name. By way of reply the servant raised his hand, sketched the characters 'Sun Szê-Mo' in the air and vanished! Another surprise lay in store, for on reaching the foot of the mountain the monk discovered that the string of coppers presented to him in payment for his chanting had turned to gold. No sooner were these wonders known in the city than crowds of people hurried off to the mountain in search of the marvellous 'fairy tea': thus Green City tea achieved sudden fame.

MÊNG-TING (HIDDEN PEAK)

This is said to be the best of Szechuan teas. It takes its name from the central peak of Mount Mêng, where it has long been grown. I hope I am right in classifying it as a green tea, but do not remember clearly; it may be slightly fermented. It was already famous in T'ang times, and fabulous stories were told about its medicinal properties. Under the Sung, numerous tea gardens flourished on Mount Mêng. The heavy mists blanketing the peak were believed to have been conjured up by Immortals so as to protect the tea trees from marauding strangers. The picking takes place between spring and summer. While in Szechuan I tasted this tea now and then, but that was during the Second World War when the western provinces had been virtually isolated from the rest of the world by the Japanese armies, so we had learnt to appreciate simple pleasures. I wonder how I should rate Mêng Ting tea, if I had some now to compare with the Iron Goddess of Mercy I drink with great enjoyment every day?

A Chi'ing dynasty record states that on one of the peaks on that mountain there used to be just seven tea trees and that a monk called Sweet Dew managed to gather only ninety leaves a year. Though this is hard to believe, the record has poetic truth, for Mêng-Ting tea has always been scarce—and is prized all the more for that reason. Other names for it are Thunderclap and Immortal's tea, names brought to mind by the following legend.

Near one of the tea gardens was an ancient temple where there lived an elderly monk who had suffered from 'the cold sickness', for which the doctors could find no cure. One day the manager of the garden happened to call and courteously enquired about his complaint, to which the sick monk replied: 'For months I have been a prey to what is known as the terrifying cold sickness.' 'Ah,' said the manager, 'there's a good tea for curing that!' This assertion then annoyed the invalid, for according to Chinese medical theory foods and drinks such as tea, which are classified as 'cooling', would be highly inappropriate in such a case. Nevertheless the manager continued: 'There is a magical tea called Thunderclap. During the second lunar month (March), one must wait for the first spring thunder, then hasten to pick an ounce of the tea growing on the central peak of this mountain. If brewed with local water it will prove an infallible cure for your complaint. Two ounces would keep you healthy for the rest of your life. Three would change the very substance of your bones. Four would turn you into a Terrestrial Immortal! You really ought to try it.'

The sick monk, though only half believing, felt that no stone should be left unturned, so he built himself a hut amidst the tea trees on the peak. Spring came. During the first thunderstorm he hurried out to pick some of the tender leaves, managing to gather exactly one ounce—not more, not less. Before long he became as strong as a thirty-year-old. On reaching the age of eighty he went off to Green

*The last sentence is a euphemism for becoming an Immortal and ascending bodily from the world of dust.

City Mountain to cultivate the Way. No one knows what happened to him after that!*

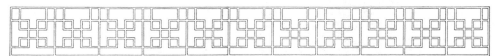

Semi-Fermented Teas (Oolong)

Strictly speaking, these are of two kinds: lightly fermented (sometimes called 'bohea' by English tea merchants) and around 60 per cent fermented (properly called 'oolong' in English). Unfortunately, 'bohea' actually means 'Wu-I,' the name of the mountains in Fukien from which the best kinds of both varieties come. For this reason, and also because the Chinese tea books do not specify the degree of fermentation of each tea mentioned, I am unable to draw up a separate list for each of these two subcategories; and throughout this book I have generally used the better known term 'oolong' to cover them both. The greatest of all these teas, Iron Goddess of Mercy, is nevertheless a true oolong, for its degree of fermentation is around 60 percent.

T'ieh-Kuan-Yin (Iron Goddess of Mercy)

To my mind this tea is second only to Dragon's Well, and yet it is very different, for it is not a green tea but a semi-fermented or oolong tea that comes from Fukien's Wu-I Mountains. Like most such teas, its leaves after processing are blackish green, their edges slightly yellow, so the infusion takes on an amber hue. Its taste is first bitter, then sweet, and its fragrance tends to linger on the palate. Originally grown in Fukien's Sand County, it has spread to several adjacent localities as well as to north Kwangtung and the island of Taiwan. Packets of middle-grade versions of this tea can be found in Chinese stores in Europe and America; it is well to choose the most expensive sort locally available, whether from mainland China or Taiwan.

    Its name points to its having first been grown in the vicinity of a temple dedicated to Kuan-Yin. It is said that a Mr. Wei, a tea grower resident in Sand County, used to pass this temple on his way home from work and was shocked by its dilapidated condition. He could not afford the cost of repairing it, but used to go in to burn incense on the first and fifteenth of each lunar month, sweep the halls thoroughly and clean the statues. One night Kuan-Yin appeared to him in a dream and said: 'In the cave behind this temple is a treasure that will last you for generations, but be sure to share it generously with your neighbours.'

Next day, though he diligently searched for the treasure, all he found was a tiny tea shoot. Disappointed, he nevertheless planted it in his garden and tended it well so that within two years it had become a shrub which yielded a catty (1⅓ lb) of tea. Brewing some in a lidded bowl, he noticed that an unusual fragrance filled the room and that the flavour remained pure and strong after several additions of water. With mounting enthusiasm he took great pains, and within a few years the original tree had fathered two hundred trees and shrubs.

When the merchants who bought the first crop asked the name of the tea, he said: 'We must call it Kuan-Yin tea.' 'On account of the iron statue of Kuan-Yin in that old temple?' they asked. 'Just so,' he replied. As the name is a good one, it has never been changed. Growing more prosperous, Wei repaired the temple and images, and willingly gave away tea seed to his neighbours so all of them became well-to-do.

Such was the reputed origin of this admirable tea. Another account asserts that the word 'iron' refers simply to the colour of the processed leaves, not to the substance of which the statue was made. Buddha Mountain in Sand County has a black gritty soil and a climate admirably suited to tea growing. The leaves can be picked in every season. The kind called Monkey-Plucked, which is harvested from very tall trees, is the finest of the various grades of T'ieh-Kuan-Yin.

Many rather similar teas grow on the slopes of the sprawling Wu-I range, where the peaks rise to a great height, the climate is moist and there are plenty of shady woods. In accordance with the manner of processing, they are divided into the two general categories already mentioned, namely oolong (Black Dragon) and Pao-Chung (Paper-Wrapped). The former is so named because children frightened by the black snakes sometimes found coiled around the branches were told not to be afraid as they were baby dragons. The latter used at one time to be wrapped in odourless paper before firing. It is only 12-15% fermented. The individual names of some Wu-I teas are as follows:

Mao-Hai (Hairy Crab)
Fu-Shou (Buddha Hand) also the name of a Chinese citrus fruit
T'ieh-Lo-Han (Iron Arahan) 'drahan' signifies 'Buddhist saint'
Shui-Hsien (Iris or Water Fairy) also grown in Kuangtung Province
Ta-Pai (Great White)
Wu-T'ui (Black Heap)
Hung-P'ieh (Red Border)
Ta-Hung-P'ao (Great Red Robe)
Hsiao-Chung (Small Leaf) known in English as souchong
P'êng-Fêng (Booster) sold abroad by some such name as 'Oriental Beauty'*   *see page 91
Ch'ing-Hsiang (Clear Fragrance)
Kung-Fu (Requiring Skill)*   *See Chapter 10
Sung-Mêng

Some of these teas are now successfully grown in Taiwan. Other good teas sometimes passed off as Wu-I, although not really grown on the Wu-I range, are:

Pai-Mao-Hou (White-Haired Monkey)
Ch'iao-Shê (Sparrow's Tongue)

Lien-Pai (Lotus White)
Pai-Mao (White Fur)
Tz'ê-Mao (Purple Fur)

Among the Wu-I teas Great Red Robe became famous in Ming times, when the output was still small. Originally it grew on Heavenly Mind Cliff, where there was a large monastery. In their spare time, the monks cultivated tea growing in a rocky crevice moistened by a spring; but picking it was so laborious on account of the height of the trees that the output was tiny and reserved exclusively for the Son of Heaven's personal use. According to a legend, in Ming times an important official sent to supervise the picking removed his embroidered red robe and hung it on a tree so as not to be hampered while climbing to the lofty branches. Another legend has it that, as those high-growing leaves were impossible to reach, the monks could only take those that had fallen, until they hit upon the expedient of training monkeys tied to ropes to climb and pick them from the branches. As the monkeys wore red robes in the Emperor's honour, seen from a distance, the trees seemed to be covered with red blossom. However, as my tea brother points out, neither story is believable: the first because a high official from the capital could scarcely be expected to demean himself by climbing trees; the second because the Emperor would surely not require the monkeys who picked his tea to wear red robes!

Red (Black) Teas

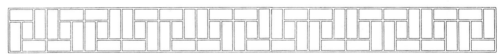

Ch'i-Mên, the most famous of these teas, known as keemun in English, comes from Anhwei Province, which lies farther to the north than other important tea-producing areas. 'Keemun' is an anglicisation of the name of the Ch'i-Mên district where it grows. At one time said to be beyond comparison with any black teas in the world (unless perhaps the best Darjeeling), it was popular with the English upper classes, although few Chinese connoisseurs prize any sort of 'red' tea, no matter how good. It owes its popularity abroad not only to the appearance of its sleek and delicate black leaves, its fine aroma and rich amber-coloured infusions but also to chance or good salesmanship, for the qualities just mentioned are to be expected in all really good black teas; some of those grown in other parts of China or elsewhere may be just as delicious.

Up to the latter part of the nineteenth century, Ch'i-Mên County had produced green teas only. The change came because a youth descended from a long line of barbers, who had managed to pass the civil service examinations and obtain an official post, was told by his father: 'Money and rank are no great matters. What is important is to learn a skill that can support you all your life.' Proud of his civil appointment, the youth paid little heed at the time. However, three years later he had to share the disgrace incurred by a superior officer and was compelled to retire from the civil service. Recalling his father's advice, he went off to a Fukien tea garden and set himself to master the processing of tea. On returning home, with the old man's help he set up factories in three villages. These, on account of the growing overseas demand for black tea, prospered so well that rival factories in the neighbourhood also switched from green to black. The produce was sold to England in such quantities that Darjeeling factories were careful to copy it and presently took over a large section of the market. Whereas keemun-style teas come in long thin strips of leaf, newer black teas such as Lipton and several from Ceylon come in a more powdery form which to connoisseurs is highly displeasing because of its similarity, at least in appearance, to the sweepings of the tea factory.

Most tea provinces in China produce some 'red' (black) teas, for instance:

OTHER RED TEAS

Min-Hung (Fukien Red) from Fukien Province
Ch'uan-Hung (Szechuan Red) from Szechuan Province

Chên-Hung (Yunnan Red) from Yunnan Province
Hou-Kang-Hung (Crane Cliff Red) from Taiwan Province
Jih-Yüeh-Hung (Sun and Moon Red) from Taiwan Province
All these will be found by those not yet converted to a preference for green and oolong teas, provided they insist on buying the more expensive grades. Of the Taiwan red teas, those with bigger leaves are suitable for drinking with milk or lemon. The smaller leaf teas are widely used in tea bags.

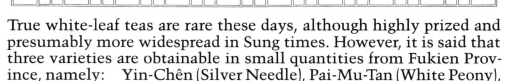

White Teas

True white-leaf teas are rare these days, although highly prized and presumably more widespread in Sung times. However, it is said that three varieties are obtainable in small quantities from Fukien Province, namely: Yin-Chên (Silver Needle), Pai-Mu-Tan (White Peony), and Ying-Mei (Noble Beauty). I have read that they are delicious, but have never had the good fortune to taste them.

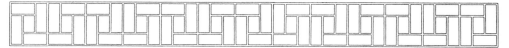

P'u-Êrh Teas

These come from Yunnan Province in the south-west corner of China. They cannot be classified by colour, as they include green, oolong, red, white and brick tea. Their flavour is quite distinctive. Some tea people are very fond of the better kinds, whereas others do not care for them, but all agree as to their notable medicinal qualities. Until the Yüan (Mongol) dynasty they were hardly known outside the province. It was the Mongol soldiers of the Emperor Kublai Khan and the Chinese soldiers opposing them who frequently observed that the local people in this remote region boiled certain leaves to make a soup to which they ascribed the properties of curing disease, prolonging life, increasing energy and doing everybody a lot of good. This tea has since been praised for its flavour and health-giving qualities by generations of connoisseurs. At one time processed into cake form, it is now often made into bricks or, more rarely, sold as a paste; but it is also widely marketed as loose-leaf tea. There are more than a hundred varieties, all of them wild yet of high quality. The method of processing is, or was, the same as that anciently used to process Fukien's *Chien-An* tribute tea. In brick form, it is marketed in the tribal regions bordering China proper, where the nomads are addicted to fermented brick tea. Besides being nourishing, it is a good digestive and expectorant as well as a general remedy for various ills. A paste is made of it which, after freezing, cakes firmly; this is held to be an almost magical remedy for a cold, sore throat or heat stroke. Another kind, specially made from old leaves—never fresh ones—tastes bitter, but leaves a lingering fragrance in the mouth.

P'u-Êrh is actually the name of a wide category of Yunnan teas, each of which has its special name. Some of them are listed below:

The trees are immensely tall when their flowers bloom and are covered by such a wealth of fiery red petals that low-lying clouds are said to reflect their colour. — HUO-SHAO-YÜN (CLOUD-BURNER)

The shrubs are less than one foot tall, the flowers lovely; and the delicate jade-green leaves have a particularly attractive appearance. — HÊN-T'IEN-KAO (HEIGHT-HATER)

The trees are ordinary-looking with very thick branches and foliage. After the spring picking, three or more crops can be garnered, so it is also called *Wan-Nien-Ch'ing* (Green Forever). — I-CHANG-CH'ING (TEN-FOOT GREEN)

The shrubs are only one foot high but have luxuriant branches and foliage. The flowers resemble peonies. Though rather scarce, the yield is good and of high quality. — MU-TAN-WANG (PEONY KING)

The trees are about ten feet high. The leaves resemble those of lychee

TSUI-YANG-FEI (DRUNKEN CONCUBINE YANG)	fruit; the flowers are lovely. When processed, the tea becomes black, but with a reddish tinge suggestive of a beauty's cherry lips, making 'people feel drunk with joy!' However, it is rare and its taste not particularly good.
I-P'ÊNG-HSÜEH (HANDFUL OF SNOW)	This belongs to the category of white tea, being indeed as white as snow and resembling the calyx of a lotus. The flavour is light and the fragrance delicate, but if it is kept too long the infusion made from it is yellowish.
PAI-YEH (WHITE LEAF)	This is just another name for *Handful of Snow*
YEH-YEH-CHÜN (SPRING EVERY NIGHT)	These trees grow in the wilderness. Their leaves must not be fermented or crushed. They are an effective antidote to intoxication and are held to be a great help to the bedroom arts (as the name suggests)—but, as my tea brother says, unless one has tried it, how can one know?
TROUSER-SEAT P'U-ÊRH	For manufacturing many kinds of Pu-Êrh teas, only old leaves are used; but the girls who pick them know that young leaves taste much better so they hide quantities of them in the seats of their baggy trousers and sell them privately.

Flower Teas

*see Chapter 1

These are collectively known as *Hua-Ch'a* (flower tea) or alternatively as *Hsiang-P'ien* (Scented Slivers). The Sung dynasty tea commissioner,* noting that various substances were used fraudulently to improve the fragrance of inferior brands, wrote disdainfully of adulterated teas, so it is surprising to discover that in Sung times even some of the tribute teas were doctored with something similar to Borneo camphor. From Sung onwards the addition of flowers to tea became increasingly common, though not among connoisseurs. Some of the Ming dynasty flower teas were like those we buy today. In theory roses, orchids, cassia, gardenia, lotus, plum and some other flowers can be used; but most are too expensive for the market, so flower tea is usually made with jasmine, which grows plentifully in China's far south, including Taiwan. During processing, jasmine is mixed with the tea leaves and they are smoked together so that the flower fragrance is drawn into the leaves. (Adding the flowers later, as is often done in North China, is a matter for customers, not the manufacturer.)

Generally speaking, flower teas are popular only in the northern provinces, and even there knowledgeable tea men do not regard them highly. Nevertheless, numbers of people everywhere prefer them. As this is a matter of personal taste, I shall not venture an opinion as to their merit, except to say that adding flowers to really fine teas and thus overlaying their natural flavours would be like spraying roses with scent! Flower teas, like most other kinds, are available in many qualities, the differences depending on the degree of skill used in processing them.

In this section no individual names are listed. Since *any* kind of tea leaf can be used, flower teas are not regarded as a separate category. Chrysanthemum tea, however, needs to be described separately. Dried chrysanthemum flowers are sometimes infused with or without tea leaves in boiling water, to which sugar may be added. Such an infusion helps to ward off the effects of fierce summer heat. Chrysanthemum tea is therefore classified medically in China as a 'cooling' drink. The Chinese love chrysanthemums and have bred several thousand varieties for the sake of beauty or originality of appearance. Nevertheless, only one variety is suitable for making infusions, namely the so-called sweet chrysanthemum, of which the finest are produced in Hangchow.

The sweet chrysanthemum has from ancient times been rightly credited with several medicinal properties, and there are some

Chinese who believe that consuming it prolongs one's life expectancy. However, this particular belief may derive from a Sung dynasty story about the water drawn from a stream called Chrysanthemum Rivulet. The Sung emperor Kao Tsung (1127-63), pleased with the performance of a troupe of palace dancers, sent for their leader and chatted with her for a while before bestowing a lavish present on each member. A very old eunuch in attendance overheard her tell the Lord of Ten Thousand Years that her surname was Chu (Chrysanthemum) and that she was twenty-one years old. When the girl had prostrated herself and returned to her troupe, this old man whispered to the emperor that a dancer who had looked extraordinarily like her and borne the same rather uncommon surname had danced at his predecessor's court as far back as forty years earlier: if in fact they were one and the same person, she must certainly be a witch! Under investigation, the girl freely admitted that she was indeed the Miss Chrysanthemum who had danced all those years ago and that her age was in fact sixty-one. 'Pray do not be alarmed,' she continued. 'My family live close to a stream called Chrysanthemum Rivulet, and we draw all our water from there so it is not surprising that we mostly live to be over a hundred years old without any change in youthful ability and appearance.' As there were plenty of people to confirm this statement, the Son of Heaven was satisfied and the girl was cleared of suspicion. The story clearly implies a connection between chrysanthemums and longevity, but whether it was in fact the basis of that belief or whether it merely reflects a belief already current in Emperor Kao Tsung's time is not apparent.

Notable Taiwan Teas

China's island province of Taiwan has been growing tea, introduced from Fukien, for centuries. Since the Communists took power on the mainland, it has diversified and enormously increased its crop and now produces close counterparts of some of the finest mainland varieties. However, in recent years several local tea factories have switched from hand to machine processing, which is not invariably an improvement from the point of view of a connoisseur. Among the good teas from that province are the following.

TUNG-TING

This originated on a mountain of that name, adjacent to Deer Valley, where cloud and mist are frequent and the temperature seldom rises above 20°C. Improved by modern production methods, it has become one of the island's best. Some say that it descends from a native tea plant that formerly grew wild; others that the original seeds were imported from Fukien. However, that may be, it is still rather scarce and prized by tea men like the tribute tea of old—the more so as it tastes bitter but leaves a sweet taste in the mouth, a quality that appeals to connoisseurs. Whether made into green tea, semi-fermented, or processed as a flower tea, it is invariably excellent.

PAO-CHUNG (PAPER-PACKED)

This ancient name derives from that formerly given to certain tribute teas packed in odourless cotton paper before firing. Why it has been accorded to a tea produced on Mount Wên in northern Taiwan is not clear. Nor is the name appropriate, for this Taiwan product is lightly fermented and undergoes a lot of firing, so it technically belongs to the oolong category rather than the bohea. A hundred thousand catties of it are produced annually and sold both locally and abroad. Some tea experts in Taiwan consider it the equal of *Tung-Ting**tea. If so that is good news, for it is more abundant.

*see above

MING-TÊ (BRIGHT VIRTUE)

This tea comes from the neighbourhood of the recently constructed Ming-Tê Reservoir where the new tea gardens produce some three hundred thousand kilograms annually, yet is not really new tea. Formerly known as Lao-T'ien-Liao, it used to be processed into various forms, including Oriental Beauty, a name under which it was sold abroad, stimulating a steady demand. (I have translated this name from the Chinese and do not know what the English brand name was:

perhaps 'Eastern Beauty' or something rather similar.) In that form it was 70 per cent fermented and so not very dissimilar to the red (black) teas taken with milk or lemon. Being hand-processed and therefore expensive, it was gradually eclipsed by Darjeeling and Ceylon teas. However, it is now being differently processed with modern machinery and seems to be regaining its former popularity.

SUAN-HSIANG-TZŬ (SOUR BOX)

This is a very new and, to a connoisseur, shocking kind of tea produced in the Ming-Tê Reservoir area. The leaves are packed in the skins of scooped-out oranges, which are sun-dried, sealed and smoked, then dried in a furnace. Purchasers wait until they want to use the tea before cutting the oranges open and boiling the contents with salt or icing sugar. It is said to be particularly good for use as iced tea.

SUNG-PO-CH'ING (CONIFEROUS EVERGREEN)

Produced in Taiwan's Nan-Tou Province in the vicinity of Shou T'ien Kung Temple, this tea has a history of over two hundred years. The old Taoist temple has recently been renovated and enlarged, for every spring and autumn crowds of people come to worship the Pole Star Deity. Nearby is Dragon's-Eye Spring, which provides excellent water. The surrounding countryside abounds in pine and cedar trees, so it is well worth taking an opportunity to taste tea made with local spring water, as recommended by the Tea Masters of old. Not very well known until 1975, it has recently risen in popularity and sells well. Some say it is comparable to the famous Iron-Goddess of Mercy tea grown in Fukien.*

*see page 81

KANG-KOU (HARBOUR TEA)

Taiwan's tea is almost all grown in the northern and central parts of the island. Harbour tea, however, comes from terraced fields in the south. There is a story that in the latter part of the last century a county magistrate in that region imported four kinds of small-leaf seeds from Fukien and mixed them before sowing. Though hitherto deemed to be of middling quality, the future of this tea looks bright.

In any case, the scenery around Manchu Village where it grows is delightful. Visitors to the area should not miss the opportunity to taste a good tea in its native habitat, remembering that all teas taste best in the places where they grow.

Some teas mentioned by the ancients are not identifiable today. Perhaps they are hard to find, or perhaps they never existed, but tea people enjoy hearing about them. Some teas still marketed under the old picturesque names may or may not be what they are claimed to be.

Hou-Êrh (Monkey Tea)

This is not to be confused with White-Furred Monkey tea, which comes from trees so tall that they look as if only monkeys could climb them and is still to be found on the market. Nor is it the same as Red Robe tea. The first Monkey tea allegedly came from Mount Ying-T'ang near Wenchow in Chekiang Province. It is a lonely place haunted by wild beasts, but in the hidden valleys there used to be numerous monasteries with monks or tenants engaged in farming and fruit growing.

According to an old story, a very young novice from Heavenly Wisdom Monastery was looking after some pear trees covered with ripening fruit. Suddenly a large tribe of monkeys came swarming from the forest and set about gobbling up the pears. By the time a few monks came running over in response to the little novice's piercing cries for help, the trees had been stripped and the branches broken, so they all walked back to the monastery with dragging steps, expecting a severe scolding from the abbot. Instead, the old man said resignedly: 'Heaven commands us to show compassion to all living creatures, and so does the teaching of the Buddha. Things come and go. Moreover, monkeys, like all sentient beings, have a spiritual nature. They have taken our pears. Well, so be it.'

Henceforward those holy men allowed the mischievous animals to come and go freely, and the latter, gradually losing their inborn fear of humans, came to regard the monks as friends. The winter that year was unusually cold: heavy falls of snow lay upon trees and mountains, and hundreds of pitiful beasts starved to death. After some weeks a horde of ravenous monkeys invaded the monastery grounds and ran agitatedly around, half-pleading, half-menacing, as though to say: 'Please give us food, or else we shall just have to break in and take it.' So the abbot ordered that bags of food be taken out and distributed to the monkeys; whereupon the animals, uttering loud cries, siezed the bags and ran back into the forest.

With the arrival of spring came the time for harvesting tea leaves. While this arduous labour was being performed, monkeys came swarming down from the peak dragging along the old bags which now bulged with freshly picked young tea leaves. 'It was as though one's friends were to come back with baskets of peaches to make return for a gift of pears!' The tea, having been picked in places inaccessible to man, was found to be of unrivalled quality. In view of these circumstances, fine tea from that locality became known as monkey tea.

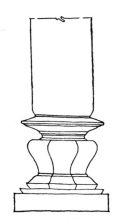

T'ien-Chu (Heavenly Pillar)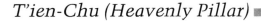

This tea is reported in ancient texts to come from a mountain of that name, but nobody nowadays knows where it is, as there are at least seven mountains with that or a very similar name scattered widely throughout China—all of them in localities listed in the T'ang dynasty *Tea Classic* as suitable for growing tea. The story goes that one of the great ministers in T'ang times, having obtained some Heavenly Pillar tea from Anhui Province, found in it a superb cure for both intoxication and indigestion. To prove his point he made a strong brew, put in some fresh meat, replaced the lid of the vessel and ordered his people to come back the following day. Next morning when the lid was removed, they saw that the meat had dissolved completely! This might be called a "believe-it-or-not' story and yet have a modicum of truth in it, for green and semi-fermented teas are admirable anti-intoxicants and help in the digestion of rich food.

I-Yeh (One Leaf)

This name is given to certain huge-leafed wild teas coming from mountains in Kwangtung Province. They are a prized antidote to the effects of summer heat, as well as being good for the eyes and for warding off drowsiness. The trees are twenty or thirty feet high, the leaves as large as plates, so one leaf is quite sufficient for making a pot of tea. Though the infusion is bitter, it leaves a pleasantly sweet after-taste.

One such tea that grows on Mount Hsi Ch'iao was discovered in the following way. The monks of White Cloud Monastery kept falling asleep during their devotions (probably on account of the semitropical heat in that region). After fruitless efforts to prevent this, the abbot decided that a very tall tea tree that happened to be growing in the temple courtyard might provide a remedy. Using one of its huge leaves, he made enough tea for the whole community to have a small bowl each. No one liked its bitter taste, but it certainly kept them awake: in fact the night was far advanced before they got any sleep at all. Asked what kind of tea he had given them, the abbot answered 'one-leaf tea.' Later they came to enjoy its cooling effect. The record states that it made them alert, brightened their eyes, assisted their digestion and cured them of all manner of ills. Naturally, its fame spread and so it came to be greatly sought after.

Another story tells us that a tea merchant on Taiwan island, knowing he had not long to live, sent his son to the mainland with instructions to bring back a kind of tea that would sell well enough locally to ensure a comfortable living for the family. The youth sailed across to Fukien, that home of good teas, but failed to find any that had still to be introduced into Taiwan. Just as he was about to return home disconsolately, he heard of a promising tea that grew in the Nan-Hai region of Kwangtung, so he travelled southwards to investigate—but again he was disappointed. Sadly he took passage on a ship bound for Taiwan. On the eve of his voyage, a monk who had heard of his predicament paid him a visit and said: 'If you really want a rare tea, I have two enormous leaves. An infusion made with part of one is guaranteed to restore the health of any number of people who drink some. Unfortunately the price is beyond your means, but out of compassion I shall give you one leaf in return for whatever small sum remains from your failed venture.' Despairingly the youth nodded and, taking out his purse, emptied a few taels of silver into the monk's hand. The next morning he set sail.

When his father heard the story, he was furious. Snatching the precious leaf, he told the youth to go away at once and not venture to return unless news came that he was at the point of death. The summer heat that year was malevolent. Epidemics broke out, claiming hundreds of victims—among them the old tea merchant. Rushing home and finding his father in a coma, the young man searched frantically for the huge tea leaf. Finding it at last, he brewed a cauldron of tea for his father and dozens of sick neighbours. Astonishingly, the neighbours all recovered, but by a stroke of fate his father had passed away before the water for the tea reached the boil.

Yün-Wu (Cloud-Mist)

This is also called *Shih-Jui*, which normally denotes a kind of lichen. China's ancient botanical treatise, the *Pên Ts'ao*, affirms that good tea of this kind grows amidst clouds and mist veiling high rocky peaks. It goes on to say that, though commonly called Cloud Tea, its correct name is Mêng-Ting, a slowly maturing tea that should be picked in spring and sun-dried. (It should not be confused with Szechuan's famous Mêng-Ting tea.) Other accounts argue that it is not a tea but a member of the lichen family with several medicinal properties. Possibly there has been some confusion between a tea and a lichen chancing to have the same name, for it seems clear that a rare tea called Shih-Jui, prized by Buddhist monks and Taoist recluses for its curative properties, was at one time picked in the Muang-Shan range. These mountains extend into parts of Chekiang, Kiangsi and Anhui Provinces, where one could occasionally buy tea bearing that name.

It is said that a Taoist recluse once came into town to offer some Cloud-Mist tea to an Anhui tea firm, asserting that it was of the very finest quality. Before he could effect a sale, in came a Buddhist monk proferring 'the very best' Cloud-Mist tea which he had gathered on another peak of the same mountain. The manager, not wishing to offend either, invited them to prepare brews for comparison. When the water on the tea stove boiled, the monk poured some into a bowl, threw in a handful of leaves covered with a whitish fur and put the lid on. After the time it takes to burn a stick of incense, he removed the lid, releasing a white mist that, before dispersing, rose to a height of some three feet from the rim of the bowl and left behind a subtle aroma. Filling several small bowls with the contents of the large one, he invited the manager and others present to taste his brew, which met with their highest approbation. Then the Taoist prepared a bowl with some of his own special tea leaves. When the lid of the bowl was lifted, out came a cloud of steam which assumed the form of a lovely girl. The figure first expanded and then contracted before finally dispersing.

Realising he had lost the contest, the monk said petulantly: 'This strange phenomenon by no means signifies that his tea is of higher quality than mine. It was just a trick accomplished by Taoist magical arts.' The Taoist laughed coldly and strode away, brushing his sleeves with his hands to express contempt, whereupon the monk picked up his bag of tea and stalked off in a huff. The dazed manager was speechless. By the time he thought of making an offer for either kind of tea, the holy men were out of sight.

Niao-Yu (Left-by-the-Birds)

This tea, supposing that it ever existed, has never been credited with particularly desirable qualities, but much has been written about how it acquired its name. That tea leaves growing on high peaks inaccessible to man or beast are sometimes used by birds to line their nests or feed their young is not beyond belief; but if, as some accounts assert, people used to shoot down the birds with arrows for the sake of those few leaves, the quantity retrieved must have been negligible. Truly a rare tea! However, in Fukien, where tea trees growing on high peaks are common, a tea of that name is so attractive to the birds that the country people can garner only what little remains after their depredations—a situation not unfamiliar to fruit growers in Kent or California.

There is a story about a married couple surnamed Ch'ên who made their living from gathering wild tea. One day, happening to find an injured bird, they took it home and tended its wound. When it had recovered, they released it, giving the matter no more thought. Soon afterwards they both had a dream in which a black-robed figure appeared in their bedroom and announced: 'I am the king of the magpies on this mountain. Being careless, I was struck down in mid-flight by an eagle and would have died but for your kind attentions. By way of recompense, I intend to make you rich.' Then they both awoke and discussed their joint dream. Mother Ch'ên declared: 'Never guessed it was a royal bird. Any way, I still don't see how a bird could make us rich!' To which Ch'ên replied: 'Why expect it? We saved its life without thinking of reward. No need to hanker for one now. As long as we can get by from day to day, that's good enough.'

Next morning in the hour before dawn, they heard a clamour in their courtyard. It started with the chatter of a few birds, but soon there were many thousands of these noisy creatures perched on the windowsill, the roof and the branches of the courtyard trees. Too alarmed to go out, they tried to make up their minds as to whether this invasion betokened good or ill. Just before sunrise the birds began flying away, and presently silence fell. Reassured, the couple hurried out and found the courtyard tiles strewn with fragrant tea leaves of a better quality than had ever come their way before! Joyfully they piled them up ready for firing. On the second and third mornings, the same thing happened. As many thousands of birds were involved, there was enough of the tea to bring in the capital needed to start a prosperous business.

Lü-Yen (Backbone Cliff)

Both the tea and the cliff take their names from Lü-Tung-Pin, chief of the Eight Immortals famed in Chinese folklore. He was in fact a historical character, a T'ang dynasty scholar-poet later credited with growing and processing this incredibly delicious tea, to say nothing of his being transmogrified into an Immortal! Having entered the ranks of scholars through the public examinations, he unsuccessfully made three bids to win one of the higher degrees. In AD 691, at the age of forty-four, he again set out for the capital, as his father wanted him to make yet another attempt. Up to this point the details of his career probably accord with the historical record, whereas what follows belongs to the realm of legend.

Arriving one evening at a wayside, Lü sat down on a bench and presently happened to think aloud: 'Ah, when shall I climb high enough to please others? Ah, when shall I attain the Way (Tao) and please myself?' Whereat a man sitting beside him laughingly enquired: 'Do you really want to leave the world and cultivate the Way?' Turning his head, Lü beheld a simply dressed old man with remarkably long eyebrows. Not only the Taoist staff and calabash he carried, but his very air proclaimed him to be a sage with supernatural powers. Before Lü could say a word, the stranger got up and proceeded to write a verse upon the wall, which ran:

Whether sitting or reclining, have a pot of wine at hand.
Why school your eyes to contemplate the splendours of the city?
Heaven bestows its greatness on unaspiring fellows.
Carefree, footloose idlers are the finest of the bunch.

Lü was so impressed that he bowed at the old Taoist's feet before venturing to inquire as to his name. 'My surname,' replied the other, 'is Bell; my personal name Cloud-Chamber.' When they had talked together of this and that and of life's dreamlike quality, the Taoist excused himself, saying he wanted to go to the kitchen to boil some millet porridge for their meal. While waiting for it to cook, Lü lay down on a couch and fell into a daydream in which he briefly lived the life of another person. The main events of his dream were: early graduation, a local appointment followed by high promotion; giving offence to his superiors and being sent off to take up an insignificant provincial post; rising again, this time to ministerial level; acquiring three wives, all of whom belonged to important families; producing many sons and watching them rise to high rank as court officials; falling from grace, having all his wealth confiscated and being demoted besides to a small post in a frontier region for the rest of his life. The dream ended with him losing his horse and stumbling about disconsolately in a snow-blizzard. Regaining his normal state of consciousness, he found that the meal was still not ready. Nevertheless, the Taoist had come back from the kitchen and clearly knew every detail of the dream, for he said 'You see that's how life is!' Lü longed to follow this holy man as a disciple, but the Taoist said sadly: 'Your evil karma is not yet exhausted.' With these words he went on his way.

 After Lü's arrival at the capital, everything started to happen exactly as if he had walked back into his ill-omened dream. Before long he firmly told himself, 'No more of this!' There and then he resigned his appointment, went home, took his family into the mountains to cultivate the Way and at last attained transmogrification into an Immortal who became the founder of a long spiritual line of Taoists.

Hsien-Yai (Fairy Cliff)

This is also called *Hsien-Jên* tea, meaning 'Immortal's tea'. There is a record stating that a tea of this name grew in the Mount P'êng area in Szechuan. A special kind of Tan Ch'iu Mountain was believed to enable people to grow feathered wings! Alas, though I like to believe strange stories, I have difficulty in swallowing this one!

Pi-Lo-Ch'ün (Jade Spiral Springtime)

This is also known by a name with the same sound which means 'jade creeper springtime'. No one knows the meaning of these odd names. The tea grew on the eastern peak of Tung-T'ing Mountain, near the T'ai Hu Lake, north of Shanghai in Kiangsu Province. At one time it was called Scare-You-to-Death tea. Long ago some peasants ordered to pick this tea, having filled their baskets, went on picking and secreted the leaves in their clothes for private sale. Unfortunately, the body heat aroused by their exertions caused the leaves to stink so foully that a passer-by shouted: 'The smell of that tea is *killing* me!' The incident, being widely reported, led to the tea's acquiring its absurd name. Centuries later the Ch'ing (Manchu) emperor K'ang Hsi (1662-1744), while on his famous tour of the southern provinces, drank some and found it delicious, but the ugly name brought a wrinkle to the Dragon Brow. It was he who gave it its present name and raised its status to that of an important tribute tea.

Tea and the Tao

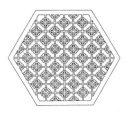

The average Chinese tea lover, though very much alive to the poetic associations of tea—jade green buds, cloud-capped mountains, gushing springs, curious legends, delectable ceramics cunningly wrought by master craftsmen—might well be taken aback if asked about the spiritual implications of drinking tea. Yet this should not lead us to suppose that such implications are lacking. Whereas the Chinese educated classes have always tended to be agnostic and therefore doubtful about the propriety of having much to do with supernatural powers, their abiding love for nature in its untamed aspects is a reflection of deep spiritual feeling, for their fundamental tenet has always been a conviction that life itself, flowing in accordance with mysterious natural laws that operate in sweeping cycles of change, is charged with spiritual significance. To be a good person, therefore, is to live life to the full, avoiding deliberate harm to others—not singing hymns or praying to a deity who, being a moral principle rather than a being, is not to be swayed by such trivialities as effusive praise or the conflicting personal desires of those who pray. However, this 'religion,' if such it may be called, is *felt* rather than talked or thought about. The Japanese phrase 'the Tao of Tea' therefore seems pretentious to scholarly Chinese.

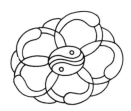

In a way I am sorry for that because, influenced by that splendid title *The Tao of Physics*, I had thought at one time of calling this book *The Tao of Tea*. Yet to have done so would have caused my Chinese tea friends to wonder if I really understood the Chinese tea art, to which relaxation, informality and utter simplicity are essential. The art, having primarily been developed by scholars, poets and lovers of beauty, is not obviously spiritual except to the extent that all forms of art express the higher aspirations of the human spirit and are therefore uplifting.

Certainly, Taoist recluses and Buddhist monks played an important part in the development of tea, for reasons I hope to make clear, but it is doubtful if they ever attached to it a profound spiritual significance other than that which they believed to be inherent in every aspect of life as a whole. During my long stays in Buddhist monasteries I observed that the seated monks were served tea in the meditation hall as a practical aid to alertness, and that the prescribed gestures for handing, accepting and drinking the tea lent solemnity to such occasions. I have read, moreover, that in T'ang times the celebrated Zen Master Pai Chang incorporated some tea rules into his code of monastic regulations—but then, solemnity and decorum are observed in all aspects of Zen monastic practice, so none of this provides evidence to support the notion of a Chinese Tao of tea. On the other hand, Korean and Japanese monks who visited China under T'ang and Sung took back with them the nucleus of what the Koreans later developed into a relatively simple ritual and the Japanese, into their highly elaborate *chanoyu*; so it seems possible that Chinese Buddhist monasteries did have some sort of tea ritual in those far-off times.

What is much more obvious, however, is that the strong connection between Taoist recluses, Buddhist monks and tea was of a largely fortuitous kind. During their long sojourns in the mountains spent seeking close community with nature, Taoist 'cloud wanderers' studied the properties of mosses, fungi, herbs and plants of every kind, and were probably responsible for the widespread use in ancient times of *boiled* tea for medicinal purposes. Later, the Taoists built beautiful hermitages and the Buddhists attractive monasteries in places remote from 'the world of dust'. Naturally, Chinese statesmen, scholars and literary men enjoyed making long stays in those secluded but altogether delectable retreats. Always on the lookout for good tea trees and pure springs, it is not surprising that they should have communicated their enthusiasm to those holy men, who, while learning to enjoy the tea art for its own sake, also discovered that as the proprietors of land boasting tea trees or sparkling springs they could make enough money to keep their monastic communities tolerably well clothed and fed. It is mostly in this capacity that they figure in the traditional tea stories.

Nevertheless, on the assumption that tea had an overt spiritual significance for Chinese monks in times gone by, I have made some enquiries in Korea; for contemporary Korean monks preserve Chinese traditions with far greater fidelity than do the Japanese who, though they freely incorporate foreign elements into their culture, tend to alter them radically in the process. To understand the special link between Buddhism and tea drinking in Korea we must glance very briefly at the course of tea history in that country. After that, we shall review typical Korean Buddhist attitudes to tea. To what extent they reflect attitudes originating in Sung China, it is difficult to say for certain, but Zen monasteries in the mountains of Korea are probably closer to Sung traditions than any to be found in China since the last Son of Heaven descended from the Dragon Throne.

SPIRITUAL
SIGNIFICANCE

Outline of Tea History in Korea

THE PERIOD OF THE THREE KINGDOMS
(AD 55-668)

THE PERIOD OF UNIFIED SILLA
(AD 668-935)

THE KORYO PERIOD
(935-1392)

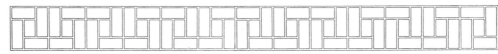

Some tea may have been drunk and used for offerings in this period, but the records are sparse and deemed to be legendary. As in China, there may have been some confusion between *t'u*, a bitter herb, and *ch'a*, tea—since the characters for these two are almost identical.

This corresponds approximately to the T'ang dynasty. A Korean envoy called Kim Taeryom returned from China with tea seeds and planted them on Mount Chiri in the south. Thenceforth both local and imported teas became available. At that time tea offerings were regularly laid before statues of the Buddha and the tablets of ancestral spirits. Moreover, caked tea, made in those days of steamed and pounded leaves boiled for a long time, was used medicinally. Korean sources suggest that in the year AD 623 Yongri, a monk from the Paekche region, introduced Buddhism and tea into Japan. In the eighth century a 'Tea Immortal' (certainly a Chinese Taoist), visited Korea and affirmed that the teas produced in that kingdom's Silla, Paekche and Koguryo regions, taken in that order, ranked immediately after the fine teas grown in his native province.

In those days there were special teahouses with the character for tea inscribed on the roof tiles, where aristocrats would take tea seated around an image of the Buddha. Moreover, tea was used very much as in China on social occasions such as marriages, funerals, commemoration ceremonies and receptions given to high-ranking visitors. These social usages were maintained during subsequent periods.

This corresponds to the Sung and Yüan (Mongol) dynasties. Tea, scraped from a cake and powdered just before use, was drunk in larger bowls than in the preceding period. According to some informants its use became widespread, whereas others affirm that it continued to be largely confined to the aristocracy and upper classes. The king was ceremonially offered tea every morning and, once a year, symbolically tended the tea plants. In the palace tea room the tea ritual was highly intricate and accompanied by music. Tea ceremonies would be held on important days in the lives of royalty, at diplomatic receptions, and at other grand functions. Besides serving tea to honoured guests, the aristocrats, like the scholar-officials in China, liked to enjoy it in a leisurely manner, especially during visits to scenic places. The monks used it both as an offering and to assist wakefulness during meditation. The ordinary people had to hand over most of their tea crop as tax, keeping back only a little which, after thorough boiling, they used as a remedy for headaches, colds and general debility. The art of tea taken over from China was a powerful stimulus to the development of the world-famed Koryo pottery, but gradually the ceremonial became over-elaborate and the ritual tiresomely intricate, so its popularity declined.

This corresponds to the time of the Ming and Ch'ing (Manchu) dynasties. Green loose-leaf tea now took over from the old powdered form. After the death of the third Yi monarch, Buddhist court ceremonies were abruptly replaced by Confucian rites, and wine became the formal drink—except in monasteries. The monks, abstainers from alcohol, preserved the custom of drinking tea which through its long association with Buddhism had by then largely become a monastic custom, so that the tea art was thenceforth preserved in an austerely simple form. As the aristocrats showed few signs of abjuring the officially disfavoured beverages, the new Confucian-style government levied a heavy tea tax, thereby compelling most monasteries to reduce or destroy their tea crop. Only in the south did some tea plantations survive, so tea drinking declined even in the monasteries, until the partial revival that took place towards the end of the dynasty. Its leader, Ch'oui Sŏn Sa (1786-1866), emphasised the complementarity

THE YI PERIOD
(1392-1910)

of tea and meditation, affirming that 'the highest state of tea drinking and that of meditation are the same!'

Lessons to be Drawn from Korean Tea History

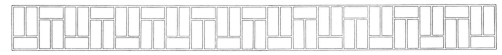

We can perceive that tea and Buddhism were more closely interlinked in Korea than at any time in China. By studying Korean sources we may perhaps gain an insight into specifically Buddhist concepts of tea in Sung times, though none of the many Chinese tea books I have read confirm the existence of such concepts. Their silence may be due to the fact that there are no Buddhist monks among the authors.

General

Let us first glance at what my Korean informants had to say about tea itself. The Venerable Sonhae Sŭnim states: 'Green tea is preferred to other beverages because of its subtlety. In order to appreciate it fully, the mind must be quiet and free from distracting thoughts. Someone who has drunk tea for twenty years or so is able to maintain the state of mind required to appreciate tea at all times.'
According to the Venerable Pŏpchŏng Sŭnim:

To determine whether a tea is good or not, one should examine the colour, scent and taste of the infusion. The perfect colour is that of the first leaves in spring; the scent is like that of a young baby. The taste cannot be described but can be appreciated with experience. Tea is drunk to quench the thirst, savour the taste, or simply to spend a quiet hour appreciating the pottery and the general atmosphere that accompanies tea drinking. There is no need to have a special attitude while drinking it, except one of thankfulness. The nature of the tea itself is that of no-mind. It does not discriminate or make differences. It just is.

As for the degree of ceremony desirable in connection with drinking tea, my Korean informants differed, tending on the whole to feel that ceremonial is unimportant compared with attitude. However, the scholarly Mr Han Ungbin writes:

In Buddhism one often speaks of the 'essence' and the 'function'. The essence represents the unmoving, the fundamental. It is associated with the left. The function represents the moving and the active. It is associated with the right. Although the left represents the essence, it does not constitute the absolute. It is through the harmony between the essence and function that the 'right middle way' emerges. Nowadays in Korea, the fire used for boiling water for tea is placed on the right of the server. However, since fire is not really active, it should correctly be placed directly before the server, in the middle. That which is unmoving—the cups for example— should be placed on the server's left, since they belong to the essence. When one raises the cup to drink, function and essence come into harmony. Most teachers of the tea ceremony in Korea today are not aware of these important points.

Furthermore, the guests should face west and the host should face east. The place facing south should be reserved for the king. In the Orient it is not customary for people to sit in a circle. Ideally, tea should be served to three guests. The eldest of the three should sit facing the host, the next in age to his left and the youngest to his right. The eldest is compared to the sun, the next in age to the moon and the youngest to a star. These customs, too, tend to be ignored while performing the tea ceremony in Korea today.

This set of ritual injunctions is more detailed than any I have heard of in connection with tea in China, but they *may* have been followed in some Chinese monasteries during Sung times, for in those days

Chinese state and social rituals tended to be quite as detailed, or more so.

Modern Practice in Korea

Tea drinking among Korean lay folk is now by no means common, beverages commonly served with meals being either rice wine, rice spirit or a hot infusion of some grain which tastes like barley water. However, certain ladies study a form of tea art, the features of which may be wholly traditional, although the preference for archaic ket-

Korean ladies drinking tea in a manner that contrasts with the informality of Chinese tea drinkers.

tles and implements, together with the solemnity and ritualistic air of the proceedings, may indicate some degree of influence from the Japanese tea ceremony. However, tea leaves (not powdered tea) are used, and the ceramic tea-things and lacquered saucers and trays reminiscent of Sung dynasty China.

Buddhist monks, on the other hand, drink tea regularly, though not in the meditation hall itself as was the practice among Zen monks in China. Tea is prepared very simply without conscious ritual, but the attitudes and gestures of the monks while preparing and drinking it have a dignity and refinement that are reminiscent of the often unconsciously ritualistic demeanour of Chinese scholars in the days of the Celestial Empire. A kettle, teapot and handleless cups are used much as they are in China, but with one curious difference. The boiling water is first poured into a bowl and left to stand there while leaves are slid into the pot along a short section of split bamboo, after which the water is transferred from bowl to pot. This suggests that the type of green tea used is of a sort that yields its flavour to water well below boiling point.

Spiritual Implications

We now come to the essence of the matter, namely the spiritual implications of the tea art. The Korean informants were at pains to stress that tea drinking involves, or helps in the cultivation of, such traditional Buddhist virtues as equanimity, tranquillity, harmony, purity, clarity and simplicity, and such Confucian virtues as some of the above together with decorum and 'cleaving to the mean', in other words, avoiding extremes. Other remarkable statements include the following.

Mr Pŏpchŏng Sunim declares:

Tea is said to be a 'Way' (Tao). This is because it is something one learns to appreciate through feeling, not through verbal instruction. If a person maintains a state of quietness, only then will he appreciate the quietness inherent in tea. If he is excited, he will never recognise the tea's quietness. For this reason it is said that 'tea and meditation are of one taste'. If one's meditation is not single-pointed, one will fail to appreciate the true qualities of tea.

A statement by Mr An Kwangsŏk runs:

How can one truly talk about tea without understanding meditation? For tea and meditation are of one taste—the taste of love and compassion, which are the final outcome of harmony and equanimity. The essence is to cultivate the six aspects of harmony; only then can one become a true 'man of tea'.

The six aspects of harmony are defined as:

Living together in physical harmony 1

Being harmonious in one's speech and not creating discord 2

Working in harmony to accomplish common aims 3

In accordance with one's religion or outlook on life, behaving in harmony with the prescribed rules of ethical conduct 4

Maintaining harmony of outlook by being open and receptive to the views of others 5

Distributing equally whatever benefits are gained. 6

Particularly impressive are the words of the Venerable Ch'an Master Kyongbong Sŭnim, who died recently at the age of over ninety. He wrote: 'In the taste of a single cup of tea you will eventually discover the truth of all the ten thousand forms in the universe. It is difficult to put this taste into words or to even catch a hint of it.' His disciple Myongchong Sŭnim recalled that while the Master was alive he never drank tea in a formal or complicated manner. After eating he would drink tea as naturally as one would drink water.

On reading my friend Stephen Batchelor's reports of the interviews he kindly held on my behalf with Korean tea people, both monks and laymen, my first reaction was: 'This is too much! The virtues they claim for tea are disproportionate!' Nevertheless on reflection I came to see that these Koreans—echoing, perhaps, the sentiments of Chinese monks in the time of Sung—had not in fact exaggerated but that their statements needed to be viewed in the right context. Naturally, the mere act of drinking tea will not induce anything beyond genial tranquillity and an almost magical feeling of physical well-being. Spiritual virtues have to be vigorously cultivated over the years. The real point is that tea drinking, meditation and the cultivation of exalted virtues are or were part and parcel of a particular monastic way of life. These three elements interact with one another, tea drinking playing a partly symbolic role but at the same time chemically inducing a heightened awareness and a mood of quiet reflectiveness.

One should recognise that drinking tea is something in itself, to be done for its own sake and not to fulfill an ulterior purpose; for only in this way can the drinker come to 'taste sunlight, wind and clouds'. This is a typically Taoist and Zen sentiment: to live is to *be* and *do* what best suits the Here and Now, not to calculate or philosophise about one's state of being and actions. Tea, unlike powerful drugs or alcohol, increases rather than dulls alertness and carries with it the essence of sunlight and mist, the spirit of sparkling mountain springs and a pleasantly earthy tang. One might object that a common cabbage no less than tea is the offspring of earth and sky: true, but it does not have the special magic whereby tea mysteriously engenders empathy with nature and kinship with one's fellow beings.

Sitting quietly attentive to the soft crackle of a charcoal fire, to the kettle's song and the sound of liquid being poured from one vessel to another, one may find that these echo the wind soughing among the pines, the musical creak of bamboos or the sound of water falling from a height or chattering among pebbles in a shallow stream. Such sounds arouse a sense of kinship with the totality of being, a true appreciation of the Here and Now. The beauty and texture of ceramics promotes a sense of harmony. The fresh tang of green tea is reminiscent of the scent of early springtime foliage; its subtlety hints at the mystery and complexity of natural processes. The stimulating effects of drinking it harmonise two seemingly contradictory elements—sharpened alertness and a relaxation of tension. The mild elation that follows is less turbid than the intoxication produced by alcohol and does not have to be paid for later as do the ecstatic moods induced by certain drugs. True spiritual life must depend on something more solid than belief: namely the direct apprehension of realities that cannot be conveyed in words. As we have seen, the tea art is highly poetic and therefore leads intuitively to the recognition of an intimate relationship with living beings, streams, trees and mountains. In this sense, both traditional kinds of Chinese tea votary, the scholarly agnostics and the Buddhists, draw from the tea art what may be called spirituality, whether all of their number recognise it as such or not.

For example, the *taste* of tea is indescribable, being much more subtle than that of coffee, chocolate, cola drinks, or ice-cream sodas. It is what it is—that is all one can say. Nevertheless, the act of tasting something is intensely real, no matter whether you believe it to be a magical plant bestowed by the gods or a mere weed. Therefore on hearing the enquiry 'What is the Tao? What is Bodhi? What is our True Nature?' prompts the answer 'Have a cup of tea,' no one reared in the Chinese Buddhist tradition or its Korean or Japanese offshoots would have any difficulty in understanding aptness of that reply. It simply means: 'There is no possible way of dealing with your question in words, but the Way is all around and within you, for you to experience by direct perception.'

However much Confucian agnostics or modern materialists may scoff at this kind of reasoning, it is a fact that even the grossest materialist is not, and cannot be, apart from the Tao. If he rejects notions of spirituality and ascribes whatever exalted insights come his way to purely aesthetic responses, well and good. Spirituality is in no way diminished by being given a different label.

It is not my purpose to discuss the Japanese tea ceremony in detail: first, because I do not know enough about it; second, because it is so foreign to the preference I share with the Chinese for drinking tea in an atmosphere of physical and mental relaxation. Neverthe-less, I owe to Dr J.C. Covell's book *Unravelling Zen's Red Thread* an interesting insight into the mind of a great Japanese Zen monk, the Venerable Ikkyu (1393-1481). It was his wish to return to the ideal of the old Zen Masters of T'ang dynasty China, that of freedom unfet-tered by dogmas or rituals. With this aim, Ikkyu did his utmost to simplify the Japanese tea ceremony so as to bring it into accord with fundamental Zen principles. He believed that tea drinking should embody the Taoist ideal of achieving communion with nature to-gether with some Zen philosophical overtones. It had to take the form of a ritual because that was the way to the hearts of the Japanese élite; but he wished it to be kept simple so as to emphasise that every action is significant and should therefore be the object of total aware-ness that the Here and Now is eternity, that every movement can be replete with spirituality. Alas, the tea ceremony as practised in Japan today seems scarcely to accord with that principle, although Japanese Buddhists may dispute this conclusion.

Lao-tzŭ tells us that the Tao performs its marvellous functions perfectly without giving them a thought. Similarly, though Chinese tea drinkers may not see their favourite art as a reflection of the Tao, this does not imply that no mysterious connection exists between them. To the extent that spontaneity is an important aspect of the Chinese tea art, that art most clearly reflects the Tao, since spon-taneity is embodied in the fundamental Taoist principle of *wu-wei*, meaning 'no action that does not arise spontaneously'.

Mountain Springs, the Friends of Tea

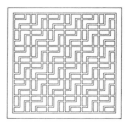

Green tea, above all others, has a very delicate flavour which is easily marred by impurities in the water used for brewing it, or failure to store the leaves in airtight containers, or by the smallest contact with any substance that has fragrance or odour of its own. The same is largely true of semi-fermented teas. From T'ang to late Ch'ing times no water filters were available, so it is not surprising that connoisseurs, who sometimes spent as much as two ounces of gold on one or two ounces of specially fine tea, behaved as if almost deranged on the subject of water. Sometimes they paid for regular supplies of their favourite waters to be brought over distances of a thousand miles or more rather than risk the slightest damage to the flavour of their precious tea. In the days when transport was dependent on pack animals, baggage carts drawn by mules (or people!), or, at best, slow-moving barges on river or canal, the cost must have been prodigious—the more so as water carried in sealed stone vessels (or very stout wooden casks) makes a heavy load. The case is different with commodities like brandy because a little of this goes a long way, whereas a kettleful

A nineteenth-century painting by Jên Po-nien of tea being made in a boat.

of water containing roughly the same quantity as a large bottle of brandy is exhausted by two or three tea drinkers in a matter of twenty minutes or so.

Lu Yü, the 'Tea God', declared: 'Mountain spring water is best, river water is next best; well water is the poorest! Of these, the first should be taken from springs where the water flows over a rocky bed; the second is drawn only from those parts of a river where the flow is swift.' Of course, in ancient times gross pollution of rivers was rare, so swift-flowing water was likely to be clean. Even so, it is hard to take seriously the (mutually contradictory) lists which various T'ang and Sung Tea Masters drew up of ten or twenty sources of 'the best water under heaven', carefully graded in descending order of excel-

Detail of the same painting.

lence. First, one would need to have tasted *every* source of water under heaven to be able to determine which was best; second, it is manifestly impossible to distinguish by taste differences among twenty or so kinds of very pure water with such accuracy as to permit their classification in precise order of merit. Still, the Tea Masters were right to insist that the flavour of fine tea can be ruined if it is brewed with low-quality water. The exploits of those ancient worthies with their apparently miraculous powers of detection provide a rich store of anecdotes with which to beguile tea lovers. One such story runs as follows.

The great Sung dynasty statesman Wang An-Shih at one time suffered from a severe pulmonary disease, so the Emperor graciously presented him with some special Yang-Hsien tea, at that time deemed a sovereign remedy for the disease provided it was brewed with water taken from midstream at the second of three main rapids along the Yangtze River. Accordingly, the minister ordered his subordinate, a Mr Su, who was on the point of leaving for Szechuan Province, to stop on his way back to the capital at the central rapid and collect a big jarful. In the event, however, Su was so carried away by the beauty of the gorges that he forgot his errand. By the time he recalled it the boat was about to enter the third and last rapid, so he decided to draw water there instead and pass it off as coming from the central rapid. On reaching the capital he hastened to present the brimming jar to Wang An-Shih. The great man received him warmly and honoured him by preparing some Yang-Hsien tea with his own hands. Carefully he waited for the brew to take on the colour that characterises this tea when correctly steeped. Presently, with a puzzled frown, he asked, 'Where exactly did you draw the water?' Poor Su assured him that it came from the second rapid, whereupon the minister said sternly: 'It is wrong of you to deceive an old, sick man. Obviously you drew it at the lower rapid.' By now Su's cheeks were burning with shame. Explaining the circumstances, he begged humbly for forgiveness, but could not forbear to ask how the fraud had been detected. 'A scholar,' replied His Excellency, 'must never be specious, but diligently investigate a matter before pronouncing an opinion. From my reading, I have learnt that the upper rapid runs too swiftly, the lower rapid too slowly for the character of the water to be harmonious, whereas the central rapid possesses a perfectly harmonious character—hence its curative properties. Water drawn from the upper rapid, therefore, would endow the tea with too much body, just as this water, being drawn from the lower rapid, lacks body and has taken an overlong time to attain the colour one looks for in Yang-Hsien tea. Thus I correctly deduced from whence you drew this water.'

This story, though overfanciful, reveals what confidence the ancient Tea Masters had in their ability to detect the province of both tea leaves and water, and their apparent ability to do so as unerringly as Western connoisseurs detect that of great wines. It seems to have escaped their attention that in most mountainous regions of the world water of high quality is readily attainable from countless springs. However, the art of tea does not depend on scientific accuracy; its charm derives from the realm of poesy and would vanish if subjected to the cold scrutiny of science—just as the moon, since being visited by human beings and found to be a dreary desert, has lost the charm it had for people who believed that the lovely goddess, Ch'ang-Ô, abides there in a sumptuous jade palace rising amidst a silvery white landscape glittering with icicles and pure untrodden snow.

By the time of the Sung dynasty the priority of spring water had become well established. Mountain spring water was so highly valued that springs became known poetically as 'the friends of tea', just as fire was called 'the teacher of tea', so greatly is the character of a brew determined by whether the water used is at exactly the right temperature to suit the variety of tea leaf used.

The general order of priority in terms of excellence has, since Sung times, been:

water from a mountain spring that bubbles over rocks or pebbles free of moss or other growths

water from mountain springs generally

water from uncontaminated lowland springs

water drawn from a fast-flowing river

well water

other

Though both snow and rain water have had their advocates, these were not generally prized. On the other hand, dew gathered from lotus leaves in the early morning ranked high but was seldom used because it is difficult to get enough of it to fill a kettle.

A tea devotee in ancient times would fall into transports of delight if he happened to come unexpectedly upon a really good spring in his locality. Of course, hermits and retired officials might choose to dwell within an easy distance of a really good spring, whereas officials on active service had to go where they were posted; it was thus a huge stroke of luck to meet with good fortune of the kind that befell Mr Li Tê-Yu, a T'ang dynasty official.

This Mr Li used to have supplies of water brought all the way from Hui Shan Monastery in Kiangsu to his house in Ch'ang An, the capital city—a journey that took months. One day a monk from a nearby temple, on tasting his tea, remarked: 'We can get identical water here.' 'Nonsense!' replied Mr Li. 'I have this water brought from thousands of *Li**away. How could the two springs be linked?' Nevertheless, he put the matter to the test by pouring water from ten different sources into separate bottles, including one bottle of his special Hui Shan water and another of the previously unknown water recommended by the monk. Asked to taste them all in turn, the monk easily identified the two, whereupon Li tasted both and agreed that the likeness was perfect. Thus he saved himself a large unnecessary expenditure.

Under T'ang and Sung, owning a famous spring could have dire consequences. Chang Tai, a late Ming dynasty scholar, lived in Mountain Shadow County, a place where the richer tea votaries bought water from the Hui Shan Spring referred to in the previous story. Chang, who sadly regretted being unable to afford its high cost, happened to discover a small temple with a spring containing water that was equally sweet and pure. Unwisely, he sang the praises of the spring at Striped Bamboo Temple far and wide, whereupon a horde of

*1 *li*–3 miles

tea drinkers and wine makers descended on the neighbourhood, destroying its tranquil privacy. Later a wine factory opened up next door, and before long ruffianly professional water carriers began to intimidate the monks, demanding free supplies of rice, vegetables and, worse still, meat and wine—two commodities strictly banned in Chinese Buddhist monasteries. Things became so chaotic that the abbot had a secret channel cut in order to contaminate the spring with unspeakably filthy water. Horrified, Chang sent workmen in to undo the damage at his own expense, but again the abbot found a means of polluting it so as to have some peace. Poor Chang scurried about the whole district like a madman, hoping to find another source of water worthy of his favourite tea. At last he found a spring to which he gave the name Yang-Ho (Solar Harmony) and erected a pillar bearing the inscription: 'Chang family property. The water of this spring is our monopoly. All rights reserved. Be warned!'

A similar theme is taken up by another Ming scholar, 'Ch'en Mei-Kung, a charming eccentric who, like many a tea man before him, refused all offers of official appointments in favour of a life devoted to poetry, calligraphy, painting, essay writing and the compiling of yet another tea book. Burning the scholar's robe which indicated his entitlement to high civilian rank, he lived as a recluse in the K'unlun Mountains of Tibet, enjoying the visits of numerous admirers, some of whom became his close friends. In one of his anecdotes about tea he relates that the South Peak Temple in I-Hsing County had a spring of pure water which the abbot used for making his favourite T'ung-Lu tea. One day a rumour started that a white snake had dropped an injured young one into the spring and that the little creature had recovered quickly. As a result, two sayings became widely current: 'True Pear Spring is sacred; its water assures long life.' Needless to say, local people and emissaries of government officials soon came crowding in to draw this precious water, giving the monks no end of trouble.

A valid point made in the ancient tea books is that fine tea achieves perfection when brewed with water from a spring situated in the vicinity of the garden where it grows. As we have seen, tea lovers visiting Hangchow today may enjoy the experience of drinking Dragon's Well tea made with water from a spring near the garden where it grows. However, the great Ch'ing emperor Ch'ien Lung, though as enthusiastic as everybody else about this particular tea, had no cause to regret that his palace in Peking lay a thousand miles to the north, for he was convinced that water from the Jade Spring near his capital made a perfect mate for it. One would need the expertise of the ancient Tea Masters to decide upon the relative merits of the two springs. Certainly, Peking's Jade Spring has the clearest water I have ever seen. The pool it feeds is exceedingly deep, yet the tiniest fronds of underwater vegetation covering the bottom are visible to people seated in the shadow of an ancient pagoda on its bank. It would be easy to believe that such water had magical qualities!

During the Second World War there were still tea votaries who made picnics an occasion for carrying accessories, including a small earthenware stove and a little bag of charcoal for making tea as their ancestors had loved to do by the side of a rocky spring. I was invited to join some students on such an occasion, which involved a walk in the hills to the north of Chungking, Chiang Kai-shek's wartime capital. All three, a young man and two girls, had specially put on sky-blue scholar's gowns for the occasion, their only notable concession to the contemporary world being an aluminum kettle. The spring they had chosen bubbled up near the top of a rounded hill; the water flowed musically over pale grey rocks in satisfyingly correct classical fashion; everything was as it should be, except that the stove let us down. It took ages to get it properly alight and then, horror of horrors, the charcoal actually dared to belch smoke and emit a foul odour! However, it finally grew docile, glowed richly and neither smoked nor stank. I received much praise for having poked it with an iron chopstick and fanned it furiously with a dried banana-leaf fan—a *broken* fan, this being part of tea tradition, though nobody present could say why.

The tea, reasonably good, consisted of small, beautifully shaped green leaves, of which one of the girls, Small Talent, put a spoonful into each of the individual lidded bowls that served both for infusion and drinking. The other girl, who chose to be called Tea Fragrance, poured boiling water over the leaves in the approved fashion, with a rotary movement of her arm so that the entire surface of each pile of leaves got an equal share. Then the lids were replaced and we spent a few moments listening to the song of the nearby spring, waiting for the precise moment when the tea would yield its maximum fragrance and flavour. The golden moment came, and we drank ceremoniously holding the bowls, still resting in their deep saucers, in our left hands and using our right hands to tilt the lids so that the liquid could be sipped easily, for any leaves that might still be afloat were thus imprisoned in the bowl.

We glanced at one another, sighing almost rapturously. The brew was a success. The tea, though not excellent, was as good as could be expected of a relatively inexpensive brand. Other infusions followed, each of us drinking four bowlfuls. While this was going on the young man, Lao Ch'ên, laughingly insisted that we improvise some poems with 'spring' as the subject. I was aghast. 'Leave me out,' I begged. 'Given about four hours, some paper and a dictionary, I might manage a just passable four-line Chinese poem—how could I make one up in my head on the spur of the moment?'

Lao Ch'ên urged me to try, but Small Talent said I should of course be allowed to compose mine in English, to which the others obligingly agreed. When the poems (each composed of fifty-six syllables arranged in seven-syllable lines), were read out, they sounded quite professional, with such phrases as 'jade-green water' (which it wasn't, but that did not seem to matter), 'nectar for Immortals',

'fleecy clouds', 'slanting sunshine', 'bell-like notes', 'dragon-haunted spring', 'crystal drops' and 'embroidery of ferns'. Finally, they looked expectantly at me. Plucking up my courage, I brought out:

The spring sang most obligingly,
The rocks did what they could.
The birds caught up the melody,
Which echoed through the wood.
The kettle sang in harmony
That fitted in quite well,
but the stove behaved disgracefully
Until I gave it hell.

I enunciated this rigmarole slowly and carefully so that they could clearly identify the English words. Making me repeat it so as to be sure they had heard aright, they gazed at me doubtfully. 'I thought you understood about poetry,' said Lao Ch'ên, gently hinting how low he rated my effort. 'I am not sure', remarked Tea Fragrance, 'that "gave it hell" sounds well in a poem.' Then, to my relief, Small Talent started giggling. 'Don't take it like that!' she laughed. 'Can't you see Lao P'u is having fun with us? Of course it's not a proper poem. Why should it be? Having tea is a time for fun, yes-no? Why make it a class-room chore?'

By this time the others were laughing too, and a proper tea spirit prevailed. Ch'ên and Tea Fragrance, in their enthusiasm for traditional-style tea, had been too solemn. Small Talent had proved herself the best tea man of us all. After that we four had many good tea sessions together, with never a hint of solemnity to mar our pleasure.

In a sense, the story of tea in China does not need to be carried any further than the Sung period; for although that dynasty came to an end some seven centuries ago little pertaining to the various ways of preparing and drinking tea has changed substantially since then, except for the widespread adoption of loose-leaf tea early in the Ming dynasty and its retention until now as the most widespread form. So the final part of this history can be dealt with more briefly.

After Sung, the Empire was ruled by Mongols for eighty-four years. Then arose the Ming dynasty, which sought to revive past glories. Under its rule a very important institution, the Horse and Tea Bureau, played a vital part in the economy. The demand for tea by the border tribes had become so great that it ranked as a commodity of major significance to the Empire, both militarily and financially. The Bureau, being responsible for the bartering of tea for horses, was put under the control of very high-ranking officials; and as an incentive to the people to grow tea in sufficient quantity to barter for all the horses needed, the tax was reduced to the moderate rate fixed during the T'ang dynasty, namely one-hundredth part of the crop. Otherwise, tea administration followed the Sung pattern.

It was in late Ming times that tea first reached Europe. Of those Europeans wealthy enough to afford it some were enthusiastic, but a rumour spread that tea weakened a person's vitality and was being exported to sap the energies of potential enemies of China! This curious belief strikes one as ironic, for a time would come when England, by forcing Indian opium on China, would indeed sap the energies of a people who should have been better rewarded for giving the whole world tea!

The tea art under the Ming dynasty closely reflected Sung traditions: its votaries, far from swilling tea in so-called 'thirsty ox fashion', liked to sip it delicately in accordance with the maxim 'Tea should be drunk often but in small quantities'. Meanwhile, great progress was made with the manufacture of ceramic accessories. The teapot remained in favour as the ideal utensil for brewing tea, as did the shallow drinking bowls called *chien* that were later to give way to cups. However, the kettle completely took over from the 'tea bottle'—a name henceforth transferred to a very different object, a ceramic canister for storing tea leaves.

Poems
and Songs
of Tea

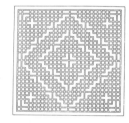

In China, tea and poetry have always gone together: to the Chinese, a tea book without poems and songs would scarcely be a tea book! There are poems commemorating tea gardens, rocky springs and romantic mountain scenery or relating the joys and sorrows of the tea pickers. Others describe the delights of drinking tea or the warmth of tea people's feelings for one another. Yet others—but why continue? Every poem or song that bears on tea has a special charm for tea lovers.

Sad to say, Chinese poems defy adequate translation: so much is said in so few words! Each line of five or seven syllables must be rendered in English by a line of inordinate length, or else by several shorter lines. To preserve the rhyme one would have to depart too far from the original wording. As for the complicated tone patterns that make those poems lovely to intone, these have no equivalent in Western languages. Then again, the poems may contain literary allusions which must either be ignored in the English version or written into the text, making it too long. Worst of all from the translator's point of view, there are hardly any pronouns. These and many, many other

Detail from a handscroll by Yu Ch'iu entitled 'Scholars' Picnic'.

words are omitted but implied, for the Chinese reader supplies them in his thoughts. The effect is like that of abstract paintings which leave one to imagine more or less what he pleases. A literal translation, therefore, would not be acceptable in English.

Of the various ways of coping with these problems, none are satisfactory. It is best for the translator to avoid being hidebound and to use this way or that, or several in combination, according to his mood. I deeply regret my inability to render Chinese poems well, but hope the translations convey enough of the original charm to make them pleasant reading. Apologies are due to the reader, and even more so to the poets.

We start with a poem by Tu Mu, a T'ang dynasty scholar-official noted for his romantic tastes and sensibility. It describes a journey into the mountains undertaken with his family when, in compliance with an Imperial decree, he was sent to supervise the preparation of tribute tea at Hu-Chou.*After the first few lines he scarcely mentions tea, but it is certainly a tea poem for it conveys an overall impression of the beauties of the mountains where the tribute tea of that era was grown and processed.

*the present day Wu-Hsing in Chekiang Province

A Tea Mountain Poem

TU MU
T'ang dynasty

*Chekiang Province and
part of Kiangsu

*Emblem of imperial
authority

Nothing in Eastern Wu*
Surpasses those mountains.
The tea that grows there
Is the finest Jui Ts'ao.
The foreman may be lowly,
But, ah, how talented
At preparing tribute tea!
Near the source of the stream,
We moored our rustic boat
And planted the flag*
Amidst the blue-green moss.
The willows fluttered
Like shy young ladies;
In the pinewoods, birds rustled
And chattered raucously.
Steps, mounting to lofty peaks
Lost in a sea of cloud,
Led to a large flat rock
Fronting a fairy grotto.
There, where we brushed the sky,
Cheerful voices echoed,
And a towered building
Overlooked a mountain spring,
Its waters palely golden.
From a purple cliff nearby
Came the fragrance of young tea.
Our horses' hoofs rang loudly
On the sunlit rocks,
As our sleeves danced gaily
In the mountain wind.

*A kind of plum that
grows near streams

Echoes of distant song
Were wafted from the valley.
Birds made music
Hidden in the trees.
Light reflected from the snow
Bathed the t'an-plum blossom*
It was good to have brought
All the family,
And good to be there
By the Emperor's decree.
A curtain of fragrance hung
Amidst the leafy shadows,
And the mountain path was strewn
With fallen petals.
But, though it was early spring,
The breath of winter lingered.
Reaching the top, we paused
For tea's refreshment.
Throughout this climb, our feelings
Had been exuberant.
Sadly we turned back
Towards the humdrum world

Now follow three short poems, consisting in the original of only forty-five, and twenty-eight and thirty-five syllables respectively. All are concerned with Lu Yü, author of the famous *Tea Classic*. This work is now of little more than historical value, being altogether too archaic; but Lu was clearly a delightful person with hosts of friends, so many are the extant poems and songs written either to him or about him.

The first is a T'ang poem recording a visit to a spring located in a monastery where Lu Yü had lived so as to be able to use its fresh, clear water for making tea. The poet Fei Shih-I, a contemporary of his, was naturally sad to find that the monastery had fallen into decay just a few years after Lu's departure.

*'Well' refers to a structure constructed to collect water running from the spring, not to a well in the real sense, for Lu Yü ranked well water as scarcely fit for making tea.

Lu Yü's Spring

Reaching the west Tower Temple,
I found no trace of people
Where nobles once had thronged,
And Master Lu had dwelt!
The weed-encrusted building
Was inhabited by frogs,
The lonely well by fish—
Yet something of his greatness lingered.

FEI SHÊ-I
T'ang dynasty

Next comes a Sung poem by a genius who could write well at the tender age of nine and lived to be a Hanlin academician, thus attaining the highest literary honour possible. Coming upon an ancient well, he remembered, it seems, that centuries before, the great Lu Yü had compared well water unfavourably with water from springs or that drawn from a river. Perhaps, as he wrote, he smiled at the thought of the 'Tea God's' disapproval of moss-contaminated tea, but at any rate by his choice of title he puts his poem into that great man's mouth.

Lu Yü Visits a Tea Water Well

WANG YÜ-CHÊNG
Sung dynasty

Hundreds of feet of well-stones
Thick with moss!
Tea brewed with such water
Would bring few guests;
Yet seeing the moon reflected
In its midnight depths
Brought me to revise
My low opinion.

The last of the brief poems touching upon the 'Tea God' was written by a lady who lived to become a wandering Taoist recluse and ended by being murdered by robbers during An Lu-Shan's rebellion. She and Lu Yü were rumoured to be lovers, as seems extremely probable from the feeling conveyed by this poem. It ranks as a tea poem only because Lu Yü himself was the lady's visitor.

An Invalid Rejoices in Lu Yü's Visit

The day you left, deep autumn frost.
You came again midst winter fog
To find me stricken as before.
I had so much to say, but tears welled up.
Pressing you to taste some T'ao Chia wine
I murmured some lines in gratitude.
Then somehow we got slightly drunk.
What else was there for us to do?

LI CHI-LAN
T'ang dynasty

The next two poems, though written many centuries apart, are close to each other in content: they celebrate the joys of entertaining good friends united by the bond of tea. The first is reminiscent, at least to me, of an essay by Charles Lamb about sitting in a cosy room and drinking tea, with cold winter blustering outside. This is a scene with which many of us can identify, but for the two protagonists there was a bonus. Fragrant tea, firelight and a radiant moon can often be enjoyed together, whereas that night a rarer joy was added.

A Winter Night

TU HSIAO-SHAN
Sung dynasty

One winter night
A friend dropped in.
We drank not wine but tea.
The kettle hissed,
The charcoal glowed,
A bright moon shone outside.
The moon itself
Was nothing special—
But, ah, the plum-tree blossom!

The other poem on much the same subject was written by a scholarly but eccentric poet and tea man who, after holding various official appointments, spent his old age painting for a living. Though he needed the income sorely, he indignantly refused to sell his works to people whom he happened to dislike, no matter what fantastic price they might be prepared to give. The poem implies that friendship and the fragrance of fine tea are reason enough to sit up all night long.

A Visitor

CHENG PAN-CH'IAO
Ch'ing dynasty

Moonlight o'er the hills
Reflected on my balcony.
The night is young,
My rustic gate ajar,
Through the woods,
My friend approaches,
Lantern bobbing.
Smoke curls above the stove;
I call for tea.
The autumn stars have paled,
Barking of wakening dogs,
Sadness of flute—wind carried.
And still we sit and talk.
The sky now lightens,
Rosy clouds and chilly dew,
The earth moss-covered.

Portrait by Liu Kuan-Tao entitled 'Whiling away the Summer'.

In contrast to the simplicity of these scenes is a T'ang poem written by one of Lu Yü's friends, but reminiscent of the most famous of all tea poems, Lu T'ung's account of the liberating effects of seven bowls of tea. (Unfortunately, it has been necessary to omit some lines which could scarcely be included without a host of tedious footnotes.) Surprisingly, the poet speaks of 'The Way of Tea' (*Ch'a Tao*), using the lovely phrases I regretfully discarded as the title of this book. This poem is almost the only use of it I have seen from the brush of a Chinese tea man. The poet, yet another tea friend of Lu Yü's, was a scholarly monk who loved and understood everything to do with tea.

CHIAO-JÊN
T'ang dynasty

*Chekiang Province

*A friend from Yueh*presented me
With tender leaves of Yen-Hsi tea,
For which I chose a kettle
Of ivory-mounted gold,
A mixing-bowl of snow-white earth.
With its clear bright froth and fragrance,
It was like the nectar of Immortals.
The first bowl washed the cobwebs from my mind—
The whole world seemed to sparkle.
A second cleansed my spirit
Like purifying showers of rain.
A third and I was one with the Immortals—
What need now for austerities
To purge our human sorrows?
Worldly people, by going in for wine,
Sadly deceive themselves.
For now I know the Way of Tea is real.
*Who but Tan Ch'iu*could find it?*

*The name of an
Immortal, implying
that one must achieve
that state to know the
Way of Tea

There follows another poem written by the same Buddhist monk which is even more Taoistic in feeling than the previous one, implying as it does that tea can replace the magic elixir by which adepts transform their flesh to a weightless jade-like substance impervious to fire and ice before going to dwell in palaces among the clouds. I am not convinced that drinking fine tea often brings about this glorious transformation, but it can at least make one feel close to the Immortals. (Some lines have been omitted, for the same reason as before.)

A Tea Song

CHIAO-JÊN
T'ang dynasty

*See the preceding poem

Tan Ch'iu was an Immortal
Who cared nothing for luscious foods.
Having picked some tea, he drank it,
Whereat he sprouted wings,
Then flew to a fairy mansion,
To escape life's hollowness.
Now he lives among the clouds
In a palace unknown to men.
His tea is made in a golden urn
By a young immortal dwelling
On a peak amidst the clouds.
How worthless Lu Yü's Classic
In comparison with this!

The remaining poem is by a Sung poet who enjoyed tea for its own sake and scorned the gorgeous paraphernalia which the great men of the Empire deemed essential for its preparation, just as he laughed at the seriousness they accorded to what should be a relaxed and simple pleasure. It begins with the first spring thunder, after which whole families hurry to the cloudy peaks to gather tribute tea.

A Tea Contest Song

Each year as spring drives in from further south,
Ice on the Chien-Hsi Stream begins to melt.
The tea along its banks excels all others,
And has long been grown by Mount Wu-I Immortals.
Last night, spring thunder sounded far and near
So, joyously, each household threads the clouds,
To where the dewy buds grow in dense profusion.
Necklaces of jade and pearl*lie scattered.
A morning's picking cannot fill our baskets
We have to pluck the finest, not yield to greed.*
Our people crush and fire the tea superbly.
Now the sheds are filled with flat round cakes of tea.
The Pei-Yüan*tribute will reach the Court in time.
Among the great, tea contests now begin,
With tripod stoves and tea mills wrought of Shou-Shan bronze,
Jars of special water brought by river,
And golden grinders from which the green dust flies.
In bowls of purple jade, snow-white waves arise
Ah, to taste the nectar of that contest tea!
How can some scholars bear to be losers,
Everywhere eyes staring, everywhere hands pointing?
To the winner comes everlasting fame,
To the losers, a beaten general's shame.
Alas that heav'n permits such folly!

FANG CHUNG-YEN
Sung dynasty

*A reference to buds and dew

*= Greed to make more money

*A famous tea garden

All their brews have merit, why this fuss?
Others deem such things important;
I take them lightly.
Let them be deluded;
I see things as they are.
Better go to the mountains, drink some tea
And calmly wait to fly upon the wind.
Why envy those foolish men?
In the tealands, youths and maidens
Just gamble with straws
If they win, they rejoice as if
They had won a peak of pearls—
And then go home!

This selection might easily have been made much longer, but other poems lie scattered among these pages and my skill as a translator does not warrant a whole galaxy of poems.

A Manual for Practicing the Artless Art

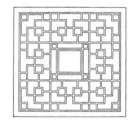

As this chapter is intended to function as a manual for tea drinkers, every detail must be set forth in its appropriate context; hence some repetition of material contained in earlier chapters has been unavoidable. For this I must beg the reader's kind indulgence.

The art of tea is artless in that it is practised with the maximum of informality and freedom from restriction. There are no rules to be observed other than those pertaining to making fine tea in such a manner that its flavour and aroma are at their best. That this simple practice is regarded by the Chinese as an art has much to do with its poetic associations: the misty beauty of the mountain tea gardens; the romantic history of tea; the charming surroundings in which, ideally speaking, it should be enjoyed; the beauty of the ceramic forms specially created for it; the relaxed contentment which attends its drinking, and its mildly invigorating effects. What is more, tea has a poetic affinity with the marvellous activities of the Tao, involving as it does the harmonisation of the *wu-hsing* or five categories of natural activity symbolised by earth, metal, water, wood and fire which, according to the ancient manner of viewing nature's workings, jointly comprise the whole:

EARTH
WATER
rain and mist
and
FIRE
sunshine
combine to produce the tea trees

EARTH is the source of colourful ceramics, tea's adornment.

METAL is the resource from which kettles are fashioned.

WATER, in its purest form, is 'the friend of tea'.

WOOD is the substance from which the tea is born.

FIRE is the 'teacher of tea' in that it moulds tea's character during processing and again during its brewing.

Water and fire interact to release the hidden potentialities of the leaf.

The Chinese have long held that tea, though a useful adjunct to ceremonial occasions, is best enjoyed restfully; so rigid forms and punctilious conduct should be put aside, as befits the coming together of three or four old friends. In the days of the Empire, when public life was overburdened with formality, it was a joy to change out of official robes into loose, comfortable garments and spend an hour or two in congenial company just being oneself. Up to the 1930s even soldiers carried personal teapots dangling from their haversacks when campaigning, so as to be ready to relax with some semblance of civilian comfort whenever the opportunity arose. Similarly, pots of hot tea or wadded tea baskets stood on or close to almost every office desk throughout the length and breadth of China, to assist in putting callers at their ease during whatever discussions might follow. Tea was the first substance to pass nearly everybody's lips in the morning, just as it was the friend of scholars and harassed businessmen burning the midnight oil, and an invariable source of comfort and pleasure throughout the day.

The Ordinary Brewing of Fine Tea

The first step is to decide what kind one wants. A selection of fine teas suitable for regular use is listed below:

GREEN TEAS (CH'ING-CH'A)

Excellent for flavour, aroma and health-giving qualities, but only if care is taken to preserve their natural fragrance and colour; hence the need to ensure that the packaging is airtight and to store the leaves, after purchase, in an airtight caddy. They should be infused with water slightly below boiling point. Too weak, they will taste insipid; too strong, they will taste bitter; so, experimentation may at first be necessary. Lung-Ching (Dragon's Well) is the best, but comes in many grades which vary in their degree of excellence. Shou-Mei (Old Man's Eyebrows) is another kind that has a beautifully fresh taste, for it is sun-dried and more lightly processed than any others.

SEMI-FERMENTED TEAS (WU-LUNG) AND PAO-CH'A

In English, oolong and bohea respectively are also notable for flavour, aroma and health-giving qualities, but their taste is different from that of green tea. The degree of fermentation varies from 20 to 60 per cent according to the brand. They should be infused with water slightly below boiling point. T'ieh-Kuan-Yin (Iron Goddess of Mercy) is perhaps the best. Other good ones likely to be widely available are Shui-Hsien (Iris or Water Fairy) and T'ieh-Lo-Han (Iron Saint).

RED TEAS (CALLED 'BLACK' IN ENGLISH)	Vary less in quality, but Ch'i-Mên (keemun) is generally preferred, especially the best grades of the kind called Wu-An (six happinesses). The water used for infusion must be boiling. The finest kinds lose some of their magic if adulterated with milk, lemon, sugar, etc.
FLOWER TEAS (HUA-CHA OR HSIANG P'IEN)	May be made with any of the kinds mentioned above and vary widely in quality. Though fine teas are rarely if ever adapted to this use, the more expensive brands are nevertheless delicious. The temperature of water used for infusion will depend on whether red (black) tea or one of the others is the basis. One can also make one's own flower teas by adding fresh jasmine buds, rose petals or the dried sweet chrysanthemums available from Chinese shops, to any tea leaves. Especially delicious is flower tea made by a method once popular in Soochow, where there are lotus-filled waterways on every hand. Putting green tea into tiny gauze bags, one places each bag overnight in the calix of a living lotus. The tea must be collected at dawn and brewed immediately while the lotus fragrance lingers. As for tea made with the special dried chrysanthemums just mentioned (ordinary ones will not do), this infusion, drunk with sugar, is a sovereign remedy for the enervating effects of torrid weather and alleviates hoarseness and the discomfort due to similar maladies.
WHITE TEAS	Hard to find these days, except perhaps for the white kind of P'u-Êrh tea from Yunnan, which some people find delicious, although its taste is unlikely to suit every palate.
EDIBLE TEA	In China, some people enjoy chewing fresh green tea leaves. In Thailand, they are mixed with salt, oil, garlic, dried prawns and various other ingredients according to taste to make a delicious hors

d'oeuvre. People who like stuffed vine leaves in the Greek-Turkish style will certainly enjoy the flavour of savoury green tea leaves.

An infinite variety of Chinese teas can be procured in mainland China, Taiwan and Hong Kong, and an adequate range (especially of oolong teas) in Malaysia, Singapore and Thailand, whereas in most parts of Europe and America the choice is far more limited. Naturally one finds plenty of China tea, in other words tea grown in China but processed to meet the Western preference for tea with milk or lemon; but most China teas are different in character from Chinese tea, the subject of this book. To the best of my knowledge the only fully fledged Chinese tea store in the Western hemisphere is the Ten Ren Tea Company (727 North Broadway, Los Angeles). There one can buy fine teas from Taiwan as well as tea accessories; however, one can ask to taste a selection of teas brewed for one on the premises before deciding which to buy. Elsewhere one must depend on what is available in local Chinese general stores. I have been able to buy tolerably good Chinese teas from them in London, New York, San Francisco, Washington DC and Vancouver. Doubtless the storekeepers would be happy to supply teas of fine quality if they received special orders for them.

I have to confess that my knowledge of the full range of China (as opposed to Chinese) teas available on the Western market is out of date. I have recently tried a special tea marketed by Twinings, an English tea firm with a history spanning almost three centuries. This gunpowder green tea has tightly rolled whitish-green leaves which unroll when steeped in boiling water and take on a deep green colour; the colour of the infusion is pale orange. Other green and oolong teas which are available from good Western tea firms are various kinds of gunpowder green, chun mee, sou mee and bohea. Of these, sou mee is

*Described under the
heading 'Green Teas'
on page 75

no other than Shou-Mei (Old Man's Eyebrows).* I have not tasted any China teas marketed by Western firms which strike me as being as good as the finest Chinese teas; but on the other hand, those coming within the categories 'green' and 'oolong' are a great deal better than the more mediocre Chinese teas, so they are good substitutes for fine-quality Chinese teas should these be unobtainable from local Chinese shops. They should not, however, be drunk with additives of any kind. Good quality flower or scented teas marketed by Western firms come under such names as scented orange pekoe, jasmine tea or Earl Grey tea.

Water

Unlike the ancients, we do not need to go to vast trouble or expense to procure pure water from far away; a good water filter ensures an adequate supply. Nevertheless, there are districts in most parts of the world where the water is said to be unusually pure. Filters will remove extraneous particles but not supply the mineral content that is a feature of water in some areas, so if one can arrange to get a supply of water from a place where the mineral content is high but free from the least trace of odour, so much the better. I am perhaps foolish to accept the old Chinese belief that overboiling destroys the water's 'life force', for there is probably no way to authenticate this. All the same, I cling to the opinion that water that has been left on the boil for long tastes flat and prefer to make my tea with newly boiled or not quite boiling water, depending on whether it is red on the one hand or oolong or green tea on the other.

Fire

In the words of an ancient tea lover: 'Water and fire stimulate each other to make the sound of wind blowing through the pines.' Traditionally, portable earthenware tea stoves were used. High quality charcoal, once well alight, is smokeless and odourless and burns with a bluish flame. A pair of iron chopsticks for lifting the charcoal and a fan made of palm leaf or some rather similar material are part of the traditional equipment. Aesthetically, the red glow of the charcoal, its bluish flame and gentle cracking sound are necessary components of the full enjoyment of tea. However, convenience and modern conditions may demand that an electric kettle, ring or stove be used. These are, of course, entirely acceptable substitutes, despite being less poetic; moreover the sound of seething and the sight of steam-clouds are not eliminated. Gas, however, should not be used to brew fine teas on account of their extreme susceptibility to contamination by extraneous odours. For the same reason the water should be boiled near the tea table, not in the kitchen where food smells might contaminate the leaves, the water or the teapot. Indeed, highly prized tea things should never be allowed to go near the kitchen, and though they must be kept spotlessly clean, this must be done by rinsing the insides and both rinsing and wiping the outsides. Scouring utensils or the use of soap or detergents may affect the flavour of the tea.

Metal Accessories

The preference of T'ang aristocrats for gold and silver tea-things was deplored by later generations of Tea Masters, who were in general opposed to more than a minimal use of metal tea accessories. However, exceptions were commonly made (though rarely for teapots) in the case of either non-corrosive or enamelled metals. Both silver or porcelain spoons for transferring the leaves from caddy to teapot were widely used. Kettles were often of bronze. (One can still buy inexpensive Tibetan bronze or copper kettles that resemble antique Chinese counterparts in New Delhi and Nepal, but these particular metals need to be kept in a permanent state of cleanliness, which is not always a simple matter if we bar the use of soap and detergents.) For modern use, kettles of aluminum, steel or enamelled metals are suit-

Porcelain tea-Caddy (with lid overlapping neck)

A tea caddy and teapot (capacity 600ml) of modern workmanship, but ancient design, made of white ceramic embellished with poems in blue calligraphy.

able, except that aluminim will look tawdry when set side by side with beautiful tea-things. Personally, I prefer electric kettles made of ceramic, the shapes of which are in some cases really elegant. Caddies made of pewter or of enamel-coated metal are likely to be more airtight than those made of porcelain. Pewter caddies made in China are especially good as they have cunningly made lids that close with a whoosh and thereby demonstrate their airtight quality.

Vessels for Infusion

This category includes vessels used solely for infusion and others employed both for infusion and drinking.

TEAPOTS

In some parts of China, connoisseurs have their own small personal teapots from which they suck the tea through the spout, but normally teapots are used to fill cups. For making fine tea the pot should be considerably smaller than those normally found in the West: indeed, its capacity should not exceed a half litre. Porcelain teapots are in common use, but experienced tea men insist on earthenware as the pores on the inner surface absorb some of the fragrance of each successive brew and thus increasingly improve the flavour of subsequent brews over a period of several generations, provided they are *never* scoured. A newly made earthenware pot should be boiled for a while in a saucepanful of water to which plenty of used tea leaves have been added so as to remove the odour of clay. Beautiful I-Hsing earthenware teapots are still being produced in hundreds of traditional forms and in quantities large enough for them to be exported all over the world. Several large mainland Chinese stores in the West now have them on sale.

CHUNG

These are handleless, bowl-shaped cups, each with a lid and deep saucer. When drinking expensive or hard-to-replace tea on one's own

A nineteenth century **chung** *(capacity 250ml) of blue and white porcelain.*

or with just one friend for company, waste of this precious commodity can be avoided by putting a few leaves into a *chung* (or two *chung* as the case may be), pouring boiling water over them and immediately replacing the lid. After a couple of minutes the leaves will sink to the bottom. If one or two are still afloat, they can be prevented from entering the drinker's mouth by using the lid as a sort of filter. The larger kind of *chung* are often used in conjunction with small handleless teacups, in which case their function is that of teapots. Otherwise one can drink directly from the *chung* after the leaves have settled. Four or five infusions can be made by pouring more water from the kettle onto the leaves.

A chung with its lid and saucer

This recent mainland China invention resembles a beer mug but has a lid in addition to its handle. Like the *chung*, it is used for both infusion and drinking.

THE LIDDED MUG

An early twentieth-century invention, the tea glass shares the dual function of a *chung* but is commonly used for pale green teas like Dragon's Well so that the lovely jade-green colour of liquid and leaves can be enjoyed.

THE LIDDED GLASS

Drinking Vessels

Tea bowls (other than *chung*) went out of fashion with the coming of the Ming dynasty. Since then, small cups have been used. These have neither saucers nor handles. Lids are, of course, unnecessary as the tea drunk from them has been infused either in a teapot or the larger kind of *chung*. Careful pouring dispenses with the need for a saucer. Holding the little cup by placing the thumb and index finger on opposite sides of the rim and the little finger under the edge of the base prevents any part of the hand from coming into contact with the hot sides of the cup and thus eliminates the need for a handle. However,

A cracklewear teapot (capacity 250ml), 2 kinds of cup and a cup-plate. The low flattish shape of the teapot is modern.

cups with handles and saucers can of course be used if one prefers them. Lifting a cup with both hands is a traditionally ceremonious way of paying respect to one's host or guest, or to the fragrance of the tea. Handleless cups, if quite small, are often put side by side on a 'cup-plate', a flat plate with a tray-like rim on which several cups can be offered to one's guests, each of whom lifts one from the plate. Small *chung*, when filled from a teapot, have the same function as cups. Cups can be made of earthenware, but plain or coloured porcelain is generally preferred, especially the beautiful white porcelain cups that are still being produced in Ching-Tê for export and that have long been regarded as a treasure by tea people.

SPECIAL ACCESSORIES
*See page 158

The tea-things required for drinking *Kung-Fu**tea will be described in a later section of this chapter.

Traditionally, there were always a goodly number of poor scholars among the ranks of connoisseurs. Having good taste but little money, they used ingenuity to discover tea-things of pleasing appearance that could be obtained at small expense. The same principle holds good today. What matters most of all is the earthenware teapot. Unless it is a valuable antique it will certainly not be expensive. As to the rest, there are scarcely any limits to one's choice. One may prefer to assemble a strictly traditional set of tea-things, or to use the handiwork of European or American potters, to have earthenware cups that match the teapot, to choose accessories of unusual texture, colour and shape, or to make a point of assembling a variety of very beautiful but simple and inexpensive tea-things. The only rules are to eschew both ugliness and ostentation and to make sure that all the tea-things look well together so that harmony prevails.

Attitude

Getting the fullest satisfaction from the tea art requires a special state of mind analogous to what Buddhists mean by awareness. This is achieved by attending to the responses of all six senses: hearing, smelling, tasting, seeing, touching and consciousness. Once it has become habitual, there is no need to bestow further thought on it.

Through the sense of hearing we enjoy the gentle crackle of the charcoal fire, the seething of the kettle which may variously resemble 'the music of the wind in the pines' or 'the gurgling of a mountain torrent'; or, as another poet puts it, 'the lapping of waves, twitter of birds, chirp of insects and the roaring of lions and tigers'. The pleasures of smelling and tasting fine tea are self-evident: the eye is regaled by the steam clouds; by the shapes and colours of the accessories or the fascination of objects strange and rare; by the delicate green or amber of the tea; and by the charm of the surroundings. The sense of touch is gratified by pleasing textures, the consciousness by all these things together harmonized by the drinker's mood.

When drinking tea alone, one may of course please oneself in every respect, making extreme simplicity the keynote. Many tea people have a favourite kettle and teapot and are not pernickety about the other accessories, though they may have favourite places for drinking tea at different times of day. Drinking in company is delightful when the others present are people with whom one feels at ease: old friends, undemanding visitors who enjoy taking things quietly now and then and can appreciate the pleasures one has to offer. Just two or three guests is ideal. Tea people are likely to be interested in everything: the tea, the way of making it, where it comes from, the history of any unusual utensils, and one's opinions on the merits of different teas.

Variable Matters

The appropriate size of the pot will depend on three factors: firstly, one's personal preference for weaker or stronger tea; secondly, the number of persons participating; and thirdly the amount of leaves put into the pot. In China, fine teas are drunk rather strong but in small quantities. A smallish pot with plenty of leaves in it is generally used, for if the pot is more or less exhausted at each pouring then the water does not lie on the leaves too long and become bitter as a result of stewing. After water has been put into the pot it should be allowed to remain there for three or four minutes before the first pouring. When the pot is replenished from the kettle, the water does not have to lie for as long as after the first infusion. As for the number of replenishments, this will depend partly on the kind of tea used, partly on the length or shortness of the time during which each replenishment of water lies upon the leaves absorbing their goodness. Often the tea may be too weak if there are more than three pourings in all. As a general rule the amount of leaves spooned into the pot is greater (in relation to the pot's size) in China than in the West, whereas the time during which water lies upon the leaves is less. Experience is needed in order to judge what strength does justice to the flavour of each kind of tea, and personal preference plays its part. From some teas a slight bitterness is to be expected, as they are prized for their aftertaste—a delicious, slightly sweetish flavour that lingers in the mouth when the tea has been swallowed.

Just before tea leaves are spooned from the caddy, some hot water should be poured into the pot and swilled around to warm it; or, if the pot is very small, it should be placed in a china bowl so that it can be warmed by hot water poured both *into* and *over* it. The time allowed for steeping may vary slightly with different kinds of tea. Good judgement in this matter is an acquired skill. After infusion, the tea in the pot should not be stirred. **INFUSION**

In the words of an old poet: 'When tea is poured into the cups, one sees bright clouds and hears a rushing cataract'. The cups should be placed close to the pot, rims touching. They should not be filled one after another; instead, a little tea should be poured into each in turn and then they should be gradually topped up so that they are filled almost simultaneously with tea of virtually identical strength. If the infusion and pouring are correctly performed, both the second and third infusions will be better than the first, which, by the way, some Tea Masters discard into a slop basin *immediately* after the pot has been filled for the first time. **POURING**

These instructions are intended to be helpful in the making of fine tea. Tea of good quality should be drunk without the addition of milk, lemon, sugar, vodka or anything else. If one prefers tea made with additives, well and good; but putting them in really fine tea is like adding vermouth, bitters or ginger ale to superb vintage brandy. The very thought makes connoisseurs shudder! **ADDITIVES**

The T'ang poet Yüan Wei-Chih, asked by fellow tea drinkers to write a poem summing up the associations brought to mind by the single word 'tea', responded with a 'pagoda poem', in other words a verse shaped like a pyramid, the first line having one syllable; the second and third, two; the third and fourth, three; and so on up to two lines of seven syllables. Though its complicated form defies translation, the bare list of associations that swam into his mind provides a fitting climax to this section on the brewing of fine tea:

Tea—fragrant leaves—tender buds—companion of poets—dearly beloved of hermits—utensils of milky jade—napkin of red sarsanet—a richly amber-coloured brew—release from tedious formality—at night goes well with gleaming moonlight—at dawn accords with crimson clouds—bridges the gulf between us and the men of old, expels the intoxicating fumes of wines.

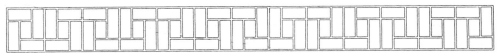

The Extraordinary Brewing of Kung-Fu Tea

The word *Kung-Fu* applies not just to martial arts but to every activity requiring time and effort to achieve mastery, ranging from Taoist physical training to a meticulous form of brewing fine tea—a form scarcely altered for a thousand years or more. In the province of Fukien the highest grades of its choicest teas are set aside as Kung-Fu teas. Kung-Fu tea votaries mostly live in the southern part of that province and in the northern area of neighbouring Kwangtung. Formerly there were talented blenders who made a living by evolving special blends to suit the tastes of individual families in the neighbourhood. Though blends of this sort are now rarely to be found, the highest quality oolong teas (including the top grades of Iron Goddess of Mercy) and a few outstanding green teas are still brewed in the intricate Kung-Fu manner, both in mainland China and Taiwan. Moreover, emigrants from families dedicated to the art who now happen to be living in Hong Kong, Thailand, Malaysia or Singapore, remain faithful to its practice. All the accessories are found in their homes, whether they are wealthy or comparatively poor. To the extent possible, the old traditions are carefully preserved or else subterfuge is used to disguise discordant twentieth-century innovations. For example, the electric rings sometimes used to replace charcoal tea stoves are fitted into and masked by square earthenware receptacles of reddish brown engraved with poetic inscriptions so as to match the antique appearance of the other accessories. Thus an atmosphere of great antiquity is maintained.

Tea made in this way, being many times stronger than an ordinary brew, is savoured like liqueur brandy and is drunk from tiny cups. Being very strong, it is apt to taste bitter. Not many people enjoy it from the first, but a taste for it is *well worth cultivating!*

Equipment

It goes without saying that both tea leaves and water should be the very best obtainable. The accessories comprise:

An exceptionally small earthenware charcoal tea stove (on a wooden stand), iron chopsticks for lifting the charcoal, and a coarse *broken* fan for fanning the stove;

A kettle;

An airtight caddy of ceramic or pewter;

An earthenwear teapot (capacity 150ml) standing in a 'tea-boat' used for making **Kung-Fu** *tea.*

An I-Hsing teapot, sometimes no larger than a walnut, but usually about the size of, or a little larger than, a tangerine;

Kung-fu pot and tea-boat

Three or four tiny cups of earthenware or white porcelain, or else coloured porcelain of which the inner surface may perhaps be covered with a pure white glaze;

A 'tea-boat', in other words a small bowl or deep saucer, its rim about half the height of the pot;

Tea-plate alone to show orifices in removable lid

An earthenware or metal tea-plate, an object similar to a chafing dish with a flat 'upper deck' perforated with holes spaced at regular intervals and fitted on to a miniature 'tank' or enclosed empty space for draining away used water;

A cup-plate, that is, a flat porcelain plate with a rim resembling the rim of a small tray, just the right size to contain the four little cups;

Cups and cup-plate

A miniature wooden or bamboo tray or shallow, oblong porcelain receptacle on which are placed a small folded teacloth and a silver or porcelain spoon for conveying the tea leaves from caddy to teapot;

A small wooden or earthenware stand for the hot kettle;

A tea table of plain or black-lacquered wood;

Pot, boat, cups and tea-plate

A spittoon-type vessel to be placed on the floor in case there is no tea-plate on the table to receive the water that is discarded.

Most of these objects probably originated during the Sung period. The fan, which can be made of dried banana leaves, rattan and so on, has to be a broken one because, according to an ancient belief,

'Nothing can be perfect unless it includes one tiny imperfection'. The teacloth used for wiping the utensils is usually white and woven of fine material. The inside of the teapot, which may have been in use for several lifetimes, is carefully rinsed with hot water before and after use. The deposit left on its inner surface by thousands of brews is precisely what distinguishes a very good (and nowadays hugely expensive) pot from an ordinary cheap one, though the two may be identical in every other respect. Antique utensils are beyond the means of most tea drinkers, but mainland China now manufactures tolerably good copies of those anciently used, and these are surprisingly inexpensive. Even tea-plates, until recently the most difficult utensils to find of all, are now on sale in Bangkok department stores; probably they are becoming more widely available elsewhere.

Formerly the Chinese rarely used tablecloths, for they ate and drank from lacquered tables which could be cleansed in a trice with a damp cloth. Even now it is best to use a bare table with a surface not easily damaged by hot water, for preparing Kung-Fu tea—until one has become expert enough to avoid spilling a drop during the elaborate cleansings and pourings involved in a tea session—is apt to create small puddles.

Arrangement

The host and his two or three guests sit around the table. To the host's right are the kettle, the stove and its adjuncts; to his left, a spittoon-like vessel standing on the ground (not required if there is a two-tiered tea-plate on the table). In front of him is the little teapot, standing in its 'boat' which rests upon the tea-plate, as do the cups, which should be placed close together on the farther side of the 'boat'. To the right of the tea-plate are the caddy and the stand for the kettle; to its left, the tray with folded teacloth and spoon. Beyond the tea plate is the cup plate, which for the time being has nothing in it.

When 'the kettle lid rattles and clouds of steam ascend', the magic moment of infusion has arrived. Now is the time for a Tea Master to display his expertise!

1 stove on wooden stand
2 iron chopsticks
3 broken fan
4 kettle
5 caddy
6 teapot
7 bowl or 'tea-boat'
8 cups
9 tea-plate (oblong or round)
10 cup-plate
11 tray with spoon and cloth
12 kettle stand
13 table
14 spittoon-type vessel
15 host's seat
16 guests' seats

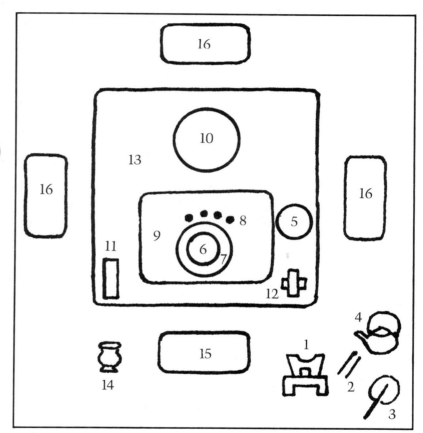

Scalding the Pot

The tea stove having been vigorously fanned, the kettle, resting directly on the charcoal or else on a low metal tripod planted among the coals, has begun to boil. It is now lifted from the stove and some of the boiling water used to scald the pot before tea leaves are spooned onto it.

This scalding is essential, for a pot used for Kung-Fu tea is so tiny that the heat of the very small amount of water used for each infusion naturally disperses quickly. Having the pot preheated with boiling water helps to compensate for this. Scalding is performed by pouring water into the empty pot and allowing it to run over into the tea-boat in which it stands, until both pot and boat are full: thus the pot is simultaneously heated from within and from without. Five seconds later the pot is taken out of the boat and the water poured away through the holes in the tea-plate's 'upper deck' (or into the 'spittoon'). The water in the tea-boat is similarly disposed of.

First Infusion

Tea leaves are now spooned from caddy to pot in sufficient quantity to fill half of it in the case of the semi-fermented kind (oolong), one third in the case of green tea. (These proportions of tea to water may seem enormous, but the water lies on the leaves for only a few moments before each pouring.) The kettle is now lifted from the stove for the second time and used to fill both pot and tea-boat with hot water as before. Then the lid is immediately replaced, and the kettle set down on its little stand within easy reach of the host's right hand. Though the water poured this first time is almost boiling, its temperature immediately falls a few degrees on entering the heated pot because the amount is so small. The pouring is done with a rotary motion of the hand holding the kettle so that the stream of water falls uniformly on all parts of the pile of tea leaves.* The lid of the teapot is quickly replaced. Strange to say, the first infusion is not drunk but promptly poured away through the holes in the tea-plate or into the 'spittoon'. This is called 'washing the leaves'.

*This method of pouring is followed during each successive infusion.

Second Infusion

This follows immediately. The pot is refilled and the tea left to steep while the host scalds the cups by pouring hot water into and over them and letting it drain down through the holes in the tea-plate's 'upper deck'. Scalding must be completed within thirty seconds, otherwise the water in the teapot will lie on the relatively 'huge' pile of leaves too long and an overstrong brew result. The cups are now placed close to one another on the cup-plate to facilitate pouring.

Pouring

The tea is poured from the pot with the same rotary motion so that each cup fills gradually, instead of one being filled while the others await their turn. Any liquid remaining in the teapot is promptly discarded into the tea-plate (or the 'spittoon') to avoid over-steeping. Meanwhile, each person present picks up a cup and begins to sip the tea. As the cups are seldom much larger than the upper part of one's thumb, one may be tempted to swallow the contents in a single gulp; but that would defeat the whole object of preparing the tea meticulously in order to ensure perfect fragrance and flavour. The tea should be savoured slowly.

As soon as the cups have been returned another infusion is made using water from the still hot kettle. There may be four infusions in all: the first (not counting the one immediately discarded) should steep for thirty seconds, each of the others for ten seconds only.

SUBSEQUENT INFUSIONS

A small chung *(capacity 150ml) and three cups (40ml) standing on a 'tea-plate', i.e. a perforated plate fitting into a vessel that functions rather like a slop-basin.*

Green tea is used more rarely than the semi-fermented kind for *Kung-Fu* purposes. The method of preparation is identical except that the leaves should occupy one third of the space in the teapot instead of one half as we have already noted.

Cleaning the Accessories

After a session, leaves and liquid are quickly thrown away. The host, without rising from his seat, now wipes the utensils with the teacloth until they are dry and spotless. The clean teacloth lying with the spoon on a little tray may have had no specific part to play prior to this point. Nevertheless, preparing Kung-Fu tea tends to be messy until its intricacies have been mastered, so it is well to have a teacloth handy throughout the session to wipe up any drops that go astray.

It is, of course, ideal to watch Kung-Fu tea being prepared by an expert before attempting to make it oneself, but that is more easily said than done in Europe and America. In fact, however, there are no great difficulties. Using ordinary, inexpensive tea for practice and following the instructions carefully, one can soon learn to do everything perfectly. A tea-plate may be difficult to come by, but one can use an ordinary chafing dish, provided that the upper layer has holes in it; otherwise, replace it with a large flat plate and have a 'spittoon' on the floor to dispose of the used water.

**Unusual
Ways of
Making Tea**

In several parts of China, special ways of making tea survive from ancient times. For example, in provinces lying to the south-west, brick tea is actually *boiled* like soup together with such additives as sesame, ginger, the peel of citrus fruits and so on.

In Yunnan Province, which borders Burma, people are fond of toasted tea. Especially if P'u-Êrh tea (now sometimes available in the West) or Shan tea from Burma is used, toasted tea can be delicious. The toaster resembles a small, long-handled soup ladle. While undergoing toasting, the leaves are shaken continuously to ensure that all receive the same amount of heat. After a few minutes they take on a brownish hue and are ready to be steeped in a teapot in the ordinary way.

Nomadic tribes, besides actually boiling their brick tea, churn it vigorously in a special tea churn with salt and butter. It is pleasant if the butter is really fresh and if one is expecting to taste a kind of soup rather than what we usually mean by tea.

Tea and Ceramics

The happy marriage uniting tea and ceramics that subsists to this day may have taken place before Lu Yü's *Tea Classic* ushered in the dawn of recorded tea history. In any case, this beautiful couple have been virtually inseparable for upwards of thirteen hundred years! There are indeed grounds for supposing that people had long been drinking tea—at least for medicinal purposes—by the time the first T'ang emperor ascended the Dragon Throne in AD 618. It is unfortunate that the confusion between the characters for tea and the bitter herb *t'u* make it difficult to ascertain when tea drinking began. Much the same is true of ceramic tea-things, as fresh discoveries are causing their prototypes to be continually backdated.

What has now come to light, as a result of widespread excavations in mainland China, is that glazed ceramic vessels specially made for the use of tea drinkers may have been evolved as far back as Han times (the first two centuries AD); at least, there is evidence that the dark blue glazed earthenware vessels produced in Chekiang Province at that time were made specifically for the purpose. In any case,

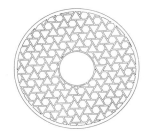

the remains of black vessels with a shiny glaze made in the southern part of that province during Ch'in times (the third and fourth centuries AD) bear a marked resemblance to fragments of tea-things. It is even claimed that one type of very early vessel, the *kang*, a narrow-mouthed jar, has remained in use from those days until now! I have unfortunately never seen people drinking from them, but apparently some natives of West China who enjoy an infusion of tea leaves freshly toasted in an iron ladle still employ the original type of *kang* as a combined infusion and drinking vessel.

T'ang Dynasty

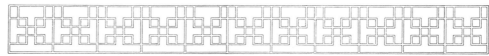

Though teapots may have been in existence in early T'ang times, they were not widely used by the kind of people whose names find their way into history books; instead either an earthenware 'bottle' or else a vessel with a long handle* was employed for making the 'soup', as tea water boiled in the T'ang style with various ingredients was called. For several centuries the T'ang aristocrats favoured gold and silver vessels both for infusing and drinking tea, whereas more ordinary people used earthenware vessels with a whitish glaze. Then a bluish* ceramic became popular. Later a kind known as 'false jade' because of its resemblance to that lovely stone was favoured, and later still a pure white ceramic. However, ceramics of outstanding artistic merit seem not to have appeared until Sung times, and the teapot did not come into its own until the Ming dynasty.

By a curious chance, the kind of saucer used to hold a teacup, though seldom employed in China until recently (except in connection with the *chung* or lidded tea bowl), found its way onto the scene at a very early date. In the reign of the Emperor Tê Tsung (674-80), a lady noted for her filial piety, used to make her father's tea. The problem was how to hand him a full bowl without scalding her hands. First, she tried putting it on a small iron plate, but as the bowl slid

*Not altogether unlike a miniature version of the old English bedwarmer

*Here and elsewhere in this chapter the words 'blue' and 'bluish' should perhaps sometimes be 'green' or 'greenish', for the Chinese texts use *ch'ing*, a term covering several colours, as its literal meaning is something like 'sober-coloured'.

about and caused the tea to slop over she thought of putting beeswax under the cup to make it adhere. Finding this too messy, she finally asked a lacquer merchant to affix to the centre of the little plate a circular lacquer rim just large enough to hold the bottom of the bowl. Thus the first saucer was born! Traditionally, if any kind of saucer was used with a teacup, it was likely to be 'shoe-shaped' rather than round, but that was a later development.

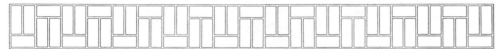

Sung Dynasty

Sung ceramics are one of the glories of old China, being remarkable for their exquisite shapes, rich dark colours and elegant simplicity. The vessel chiefly employed for infusing and drinking tea was the *chien*, a wide, shallow bowl. Those from Chien-An in Fukien, made of black glazed ceramic with the pattern called 'rabbit's fur' were highly prized; but there were in all five famous kilns scattered through various provinces, each of which made its own types of *chien*. Black remained the favourite colour, for Sung people preferred white tea and enjoyed the contrast. Other colours favoured for *chien* were blue, bluish-white and that of molasses. It is now reported that prototypes of the porcelain later used to manufacture exquisite white Ching-Tê cups, and also of the naturally coloured earthenware such as that of the famous I-Hsing teapots may have existed in T'ang times, but they had a long way to go before becoming the objects most sought after by votaries of the tea art. Meanwhile, the more typically Sung products reached great heights of excellence, as evidenced by the surviving pieces in various art collections throughout the world. Happily, they were to have great influence on Korean ceramics, which continued to draw inspiration from these masterpieces until comparatively recent times. The emphasis was on what scholarly Chinese call *yu-ya* (literally 'deep elegance'). To be *yu-ya* a vessel must be graceful in shape, sober in colour and the fruit of such

*A Sung dynasty
ceramic bowl with
silver rim and rabbit's-
fur pattern.
See page 16.*

austerity of taste as vehemently to preclude elaborate or ostentatious decoration.

Sung enthusiasm for excellence in ceramics and in tea is well illustrated by the following story. In Hu-Chou there dwelt a gentleman whose tea accessories were objects of great beauty and who had the finest teas sent to him as soon as they appeared on the market. One day a beggar came to his door and said in cultivated accents greatly at odds with his appearance: 'Sir, I have heard that your tea is superb. Permit this unworthy person to judge if it fully deserves its high reputation.' Somewhat taken aback, the householder gave orders that a pot of tea be brewed for the beggar. Amazingly, the ragged fellow was not overly impressed, for he said: 'Well, well, it is drinkable, but the aroma is too faint. I humbly opine that your beautiful teapot, being rather new, is incapable of adding the exquisite touch afforded by a teapot which has been in constant use for several decades.' 'How do you come to know about that?' replied the rich man. 'You don't look like a connoisseur.'

'Ah, but I am,' smiled the other. 'Once I was rich enough to indulge an extravagant taste for precious teas, but gradually I exhausted my whole fortune on them. One by one I sold my possessions, retaining only one object, a teapot with which I cannot bear to part.' Taking it from the pocket of his robe, he added, 'Perhaps you will deign to sample its excellence?'

It was indeed a lovely pot which, during all its years of use, had been properly cherished so that its pores contained a rich deposit of past brews that enhanced the flavour of even the finest of teas. Of course, the rich man longed to have it for his own, so he offered a tantalising price. 'Ah, no!' cried the beggar. 'A thousand gold pieces would not tempt me. Instead you may have a half share in it for a mere five hundred ounces of silver. If you agree, I shall leave it here, and come once a day to enjoy a brew.' Joyfully, the rich man consented. Thereafter they brewed excellent tea day after day and enjoyed it together.

It is hard to believe that even the most ardent of tea lovers would spend a great fortune on gratifying his passion. Perhaps the story was written tongue in cheek to illustrate the saying that 'The price of one pot of rich man's tea would keep a beggar for half a year', but it could be true, as may be gauged from a modern story related towards the end of this chapter.

Yüan (Mongol) Dynasty

During the rule of this short-lived dynasty, although extraordinary progress was achieved in the realm of natural sciences, the arts failed to follow suit. The tea drinkers of that epoch favoured several types of *chien*—bluish, blue and white, or varicoloured.

Ming Dynasty

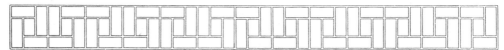

It was in early Ming times that the *p'ing* or bottle finally gave way to the kettle, and the *chien* to the teapot; the latter's popularity naturally led to a great demand for teacups. The word for 'bottle' remained in use but thenceforth denoted a kind of ceramic tea caddy. Extensive experiments were made in the manufacture of ceramics, which carried them to new heights of elegance and splendour. The beautiful pale green wave called celadon dates from this time. Furthermore, the I-Hsing kilns entered upon an era of greatness which has continued until today. It is said that a monk from Golden Sand Monastery, lying some thirteen miles south-east of I-Hsing, being fond of pottery and having many friends among the clay diggers, one day took a handful of fine clay, refined it three times, and made a teapot— a direct forerunner of the countless I-Hsing teapots destined to capture the hearts of generations of tea people all over China.* The discovery of how to make them with clays of many different colours is, like

*They are sometimes called Yang-Hsien teapots, in honour of the famous tribute tea of that name.

the invention of teapots, attributed to a Buddhist monk living in that area. One account runs as follows.

Long, long ago a certain monk used to travel from village to village trying to find buyers for something he called 'riches and honour soil'. At last some villagers asked to see it, so he took them to Green Dragon Mountain, Yellow Dragon Mountain, White Jewel-Stone Mountain and several other places, pointing here and there and saying: 'All the earth in these hills is "wealthy-cave soil'. Dig and see for yourselves!' They did so and discovered the clays of seven colours from which 'seven-colour earthenware' has since been made. Doubtless those peasants became rich. This account is legendary, but tea enthusiasts never tire of listening to half-fabulous stories, especially if they have a certain poetic truth.

Ching (Manchu) Dynasty

During the Ch'ing period the many new varieties of ceramics that appeared under Ming were developed and expanded. The output was greater than before, much of it superb; but in the latter part of the dynasty there was a tendency towards overembellishment both in porcelain and in the other arts that curiously parallels the contemporary decadence of Victorian England. Furthermore, huge quantities of ceramics destined for export, besides being on the whole of poorer quality, were modified to suit the tastes of various southeast Asian and Western countries. On the other hand, a demand grew up in the West for really fine quality Chinese porcelain, particularly celadon. Owing to various misfortunes suffered by China, many of the finest surviving specimens of Chinese ceramics of all dynasties are now to be found in collections in Europe and America.

Throughout the dynasty tea people remained faithful to their fondness for I-Hsing teapots and loved to use them with Ching-Tê teacups, especially the white ones. There were, of course, many other types of tea-things, including blue and white, celadon, variegated, gold-coloured porcelain from Kuangtung, lacquer-coated ceramics from Fukien and so on. A standard for judging porcelain teacups enunciated in the reign of Yung Chêng (1723-36) has remained the ideal ever since. They should be thin as an eggshell, have a whiteness of resplendent purity, respond to a light blow with a bell-like note and shine like a mirror. Of special interest are the cups and teapots made for the use of tea connoisseurs in Thailand during this dynasty. They are of fine, highly polished earthenware, the rims, spouts and lids being protected against chipping by narrow bands of metal. One still finds them in Bangkok shops, but they are now becoming rather expensive.

Taking the Ming and Ch'ing dynasties together, one may speak of them as the golden age of Chinese ceramics. Pale green celadon; blue*and white porcelain of which the gorgeous blue was the fruit of a process learnt from Central Asia, decorated porcelain with up to seven glowing colours; the so-called ox-blood porcelain whose ugly name belies the richness of a colour unequalled by the splendour of dark rubies; Ching-Tê porcelain with a dazzling whiteness of unbelievable purity; the many kinds of glazed earthenware that preserve the natural hues of a vast range of clays; the hundreds of varied shapes, simple, intricate, elegant, austere, bizarre, grotesque; and the innumerable forms of decoration achieved by the calligrapher's or artist's brush or by adorning the surface of the vessels with lacquer, enamel, precious metals and the like—all of these together reveal levels of artistry, creativity, skilled workmanship and imagination that in all probability will never be excelled. The part played by tea in these developments would be hard to exaggerate; there was an inexhaustible demand from aristocratic and scholarly tea men for teapots, teacups and caddies that would combine the qualities of uniqueness and beauty.

Nor should it be forgotten that all the books ever written on

*In this context 'blue' unequivocally means 'blue'

Chinese ceramics jointly cover only a part of the whole. While it is true that the most outstanding developments have been more or less fully documented by Chinese and Western experts, it is also true that the beauties of many ceramic objects have been left unsung, just because such objects were too plentiful to excite notice. All over China there used to be kilns whose products, though scarcely known beyond their immediate localities, would be recognised today as having considerable merit. To take just one example at random, during the 1930s, while spending a year in Yunnan Province, I came upon a kind of greyish earthenware teacup of which the inner surface and a part of the outer surface were covered with an apple-green glaze that petered out in an irregular line towards the base. It was selling at perhaps half a US cent per cup. Though regarded as purely utilitarian, it had been made by the same process and with the same materials used in the same manner for many centuries. I thought it charming, but having little understanding of the devastating historical changes soon to be occasioned by the war, did not think to carry those I bought away. Ah, if I had some now I believe I should have the pleasure of refusing some very handsome offers for them! I am sure this story could be duplicated by residents in many of China's thousands of provinces. Such delightful cups and bowls were like flowers 'born to blush unseen and waste their sweetness on the desert air'!

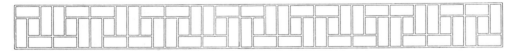

1912-1949

After the fall of the Ch'ing dynasty in 1911 came a time of revolution and civil commotion and a long, exhausting war with Japan. The manufacture of ceramics continued to the extent possible, but no striking developments occurred. However, before going on to relate what has happened since the Communist Revolution I should like to tell a story pertaining to the 1930s which appears in one of the books by my Tea Brother. As he heard it from someone involved in the events described, there is no reason to doubt that it is factual. For me, as for him, its special interest lies in its pointing to the possible truth of the barely credible Sung legend about the beggar and his teapot, for it reveals the lengths to which tea people will go to preserve a pot they have cherished over the years.

A certain military man was posted to Hsü-Chou, to the north of Shanghai. His commanding officer billeted himself on the house of a wealthy family. The owner being absent at the time, his son did the honours and gave his guest a welcoming banquet followed by a tea session. The teapot possessed such charm that the officer, taking it in his hands to examine it more closely, could hardly bear to put it down. Observing his interest, the young host said politely, 'My dear sir, you are most welcome to keep it,'—an offer which the other un-blushingly accepted. When the young man's father returned and missed his favourite teapot, he understandably came near to choking with rage and grief. But what could he do? How does one demand the return of a gift freely made to a guest? In the end he ordered his son to present, as an unsolicited gift, a thousand silver dollars to the officer (who had meanwhile moved into other quarters) and then to implore him to return the teapot—which happily was done.

Modern (1949 Onwards)

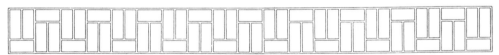

In mainland China today, the northerners make tea in what by Chinese standards are large teapots, for in the north where apart from Peking, there have not been many tea connoisseurs during the last few centuries, the general preference is for flower tea, which lends itself to infusion in relatively large teapots. In the Shanghai area and farther south a new utensil, a tea mug with handle and lid that combines the uses of teapot and teacup, has come into vogue. Though far from elegant, it suits a society where, as there are now a good many

Left: A modern
'celadon' teaset. Pots
of this shape were
formerly used for wine,
but some T'ang
dynasty teapots
looked rather like this.

Right: A modern
square teapot
(capacity 500ml) of
traditional design.

people who either cannot afford or do not care for tea, those who enjoy it must brew it for themselves and wash up with the minimum of trouble. In the more westerly provinces, however, the traditional *chung* is still popular. Like the modern tea mug, it is used both for infusion and drinking. In and around Shanghai, lidded glasses are sometimes used for green tea. However, tea connoisseurs are still faithful to I-Hsing teapots and Ching-Tê cups or have taken to using modern celadon.

Fortunately for Westerners who would like to enjoy tea made in some of the traditional ways described in this book, mainland China has now resumed production (and export) of various kinds of traditional tea accessory, including I-Hsing teapots, Cheng-Tê, teacups (both white and coloured) and sets of celadon teapots and cups. Indeed the manufacture of celadon at Shang-Shan, not far from Shanghai, has been resumed after an interval of three hundred years.

Products of the I-Hsing Kilns

I-Hsing is situated in Kiangsu, near the west bank of the T'ai-Hu Lake and across from Soochow, a city long famed for its canals, humped bridges, landscape gardens, handsome teahouses, cultured scholars and lovely girls. Between the city and the lake is a region full of hills and streams where ceramic clay occurs in many colours. The most typical of the earthenware teapots called Yang-Hsien of I-Hsing are of sober, earthy hues, lightly engraved with a line or two of masterly calligraphy. The very tiny ones, being intended for *Kung-Fu* tea, look as though they have been made for doll's tea parties, for the principle is that the smaller the pot the less will the subtle aroma be dispersed; moreover, as large pots are not emptied by one pouring, the tea leaves tend to stew. The subdued colours and varied shapes of I-Hsing teapots are as fascinating as a heap of gems or a collection of precious curios.

It was not until after the middle of the Ming dynasty (the early sixteenth century) that I-Hsing teapots suddenly achieved unique fame. Though hundreds of different shapes have been created since then, those dating from the sixteenth to the nineteenth centuries are still being reproduced. They are generally classified according to shape in four categories:

····• 'geometric' (spherical, cylindrical, cubic, rectangular, etc.
····• 'naturalistic' (resembling tree trunks, plants, flowers, etc.
····• 'ribbed' or 'segmented' (stylized flower, fruit and plantshapes, for example resembling melons, pumpkins or peaches)
····• 'miniature' (the tiny pots used for *Kung-fu* tea).

A modern I-Hsing teapot (capacity 400ml) of traditional design.

Most have the handle at one end, the spout at the other, but some have handles on top which are joined to the pot above the spout and at a corresponding point opposite. The colour is usually one of a wide range of natural clay colours—brown, yellowish, reddish, green, blue or purplish. Some are unglazed, some (especially those destined for Thailand) highly polished, but in every case the colours are charming. Some are severely simple in shape, while others have decorations made by the hand of the potter in the form of openwork floral patterns or patterns in bas-relief; the spout may be formed like a dragon's head, the knob of the lid resemble a small frog or lizard, the handle looks like the stem of a plant and so on.

However, in the Ch'ing period more elaborate forms of surface decoration became popular. Appliqué work, stamped designs, glazes, coloured enamels and even lacquer were applied to pots with an otherwise plain surface. In the Chia Ch'ing Emperor's reign (1796-1820), under the influence of the famous scholar and pot designer Ch'ên Man-Shing, very plain teapots with fragments of poetry incised in scholarly calligraphy became popular. Most of these types can still be found. The earlier teapots have the name of the potter inscribed on the bottom. Later it became the fashion to reproduce both the potter's name and his personal seal. Towards the end of the nineteenth century, when the manufacture of these teapots became more commercialised, names of companies started appearing on the base.

Though I-Hsing pots produced in the present century are rarely of the same high quality as the best of those made earlier, most are more or less close copies of characteristic Ming and Ch'ing shapes, so they are still very beautiful. It is a pleasure to find in the modern world articles which are traditional in form, truly beautiful and yet well within the means of nearly everybody. Recent production of new shapes has been going ahead, but these also tend to have the same quiet elegance as the earlier teapots.

To enjoy good Chinese tea one is not obliged to have Chinese accessories, though personally, as a traditionalist, I prefer them. However, the fact remains that by no means everybody can immediately lay their hands on an I-Hsing teapot and a set of white porcelain Cheng-Tê cups, cups of green or white jade or a pot and cups of modern celadon, so unless one lives near a city where the local Chinese stores have these things on sale alternatives must be found. Some people have the ingenuity to acquire, or create, simple objects of real beauty such as cups and a tray carved out of gnarled roots, driftwood or hollow bamboo—the variety of possibilities is endless. What matters is that all the accessories used should harmonise with one another, whether made of similar or contrasting materials. These days skilled potters can be found in most localities of the world, and some of their cups and teapots betray a Chinese or Japanese influence. The only difficulty is that of recognising on sight exactly which pot cries out to be taken home and cherished like a jewel of great price.

Though I am all for simplicity, I do believe that tea is at its best in the company of beautiful—not necessarily expensive—accessories, just as certain people famous for witty conversation or moving oratory excel themselves when beautiful and intelligent women hang upon their words. A combination of fine tea, enchanting objects and soothing surroundings exerts a therapeutic effect by washing away the corrosive strains and stresses of modern life. One may go further and come to recognise that this combination, in some circumstances, induces a mood that is spiritually refreshing; for as tea, beauty and quiet surroundings are all conducive to peaceful contemplation and to a relaxed, genial state of mind, they may lead to the dawning of an experience which magically reveals the close kinship obtaining between the individual and the totality of his surroundings. No wonder Zen Masters, when confronted by unnecessarily abstruse questions, tend to answer smilingly: 'Have a cup of tea'!

TEA AND CERAMICS   183

On discovering that tea fosters the special attitudes involved in following the Way, we shall want our tea sessions, whether solitary or in company, to be set refreshingly apart from more humdrum activities. Since appropriate objects, surroundings and atmosphere all help to emphasise that feeling of withdrawal into a world of beauty, some expenditure of time, thought and money on collecting a heart-satisfying set of tea-things would seem to be exceedingly worth while.

One of the dilemmas familiar to Chinese tea people is that on the one hand it is delightful to drink tea in a forest, on the shores of a lake, or perched high upon a mountain side; but, on the other, one does not wish to take the risk of carrying breakable ceramic tea-things on such an outing. Of course there are picnic baskets with plastic mugs for such occasions, but—fine tea and plastic? Ugh! The Chinese solution is to have a basket in which the tea-things nestle amidst thick wadding. The wadding, usually made of cotton wool covered with cloth, has a series of specially shaped holes into which the teapot and cups, being of exactly the same shape and proportions as the holes, fit snugly. Normally, picnics demand a minimum of impediments, but tea people's picnics are an exception. Taiwan's Tea Master Chang T'ieh-Chün recommends going for a walk in the wilderness carrying a portable tea stove, a supply of good charcoal, a pair of iron tongs, a fan, a caddy of delectable tea, cups and teapot and (if necessary) a supply of pure water. This kind of tea party inspired Sung poets to compose who knows how many charming verses. It is a joy to spend an afternoon or evening far from the hurly-burly of the modern world. By choosing an ambience of pine trees, curious rock formations, mountain streams, sparkling sunshine, sunset clouds or moonlight, we can conjure up the atmosphere beloved of Sung Tea Masters. Where else would tea taste quite so delicious as in such poetic surroundings?

Tea
and Health

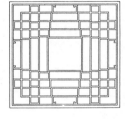

Ever since Lu Yü wrote the first of all ten books twelve hundred years ago, green and semi-fermented teas have been valued for their health-promoting qualities. Until not long ago the Chinese healing art received scant attention in the West, but the picture is now changing—for three good reasons. Firstly, the success of acupuncture has demonstrated that a system of healing based on invisible 'points' and 'centres', undiscoverable by eye or microscope, is effective; secondly, the Chinese notion of prescribing for the *patient* (that is for the particular condition of each individual body-mind at a given time rather than for the general nature of the *ailment*) is gaining ground and leading to some preference for holistic healing in the West; and thirdly, remedies made from substances (mostly herbal) found in their natural form are less likely than chemical and synthetic medicines to cause injurious side effects. Experience in places such as Hong Kong, where good Chinese-style and Western-style physicians are abundant, reveals that for certain ailments (notably high blood pressure and a number of internal disorders) Chinese treatment can be effective where Western treatment fails.

Traditionally, green tea has been classified in China as a 'cooling' beverage. That it is almost invariably drunk hot is not the point at issue, for in a Chinese medical context 'cooling' and 'heating' do not refer to the effects of a substance on body temperature but to two contrasting categories of effects wrought upon the bodily organs. Probably 'assuaging' and 'stimulating' come nearer in meaning—each of these actions being desirable or contraindicated in certain situations. According to ancient texts, the main curative, tonic and prophylactic effects of drinking tea are as follows.

Traditional Claims

Tea drinking is reputed to:

1. increase blood flow to all parts of the body;
2. stimulate clear thinking and mental alertness;
3. speed the elimination of alcohol and other harmful substances (fats and nicotine, for example) from the bodily organs;
4. increase the body's powers of resistance to a wide range of diseases;
5. accelerate the metabolism and the intake of oxygen by the bodily organs;
6. prevent tooth decay;
7. have a cleansing and invigorating effect upon the skin, which assists in the preservation of a youthful appearance;
8. prevent or slow down the onset of anaemia;
9. clear the urine and facilitate its flow;
10. benefit and brighten the eyes;
11. combat the effects of summer heat;
12. assist the digestion;
13. ease discomfort in the limbs and joints;

14. decrease harmful secretion of mucus;
15. assuage thirst;
16. banish fatigue or fits of depression, raising the spirits and inducing a general feeling of well being;
17. prolong the life span of the individual.

This is an impressive list. However, modern medical research in Japan and elsewhere has confirmed the validity of most of these claims, while refuting only one or two. There seems to be no evidence that tea decreases the inroads of tooth decay. As for prolonging the life span, a goal to which generations of Taoists devoted their lifelong research (inadvertently poisoning more than one emperor in the process!), there is no evidence that tea directly promotes longevity; but clearly it does so indirectly, by performing its various curative and preventive functions. It should nevertheless be noted that in all but a few cases these virtues belong specifically to green and partially fermented teas; black tea, in the course of being fully fermented, has been subjected to a process that reduces some of the health-giving properties of tea in its green or semi-green state.

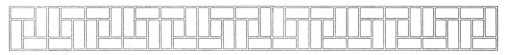

The Findings of Modern Research

Science has found that the composition of tea includes the following substances.

CAFFEINE

This stimulant, if not used to excess, promotes alertness. People who feel drowsy for a long time after they wake up will find that a few cups of tea will put this right. Those who must work late into the night will find tea effective in keeping them alert; but of course, for that very reason, unless one is a 'hardened tea drinker' it is better to avoid drinking much of it during the hours before bedtime.

Caffeine also assists in the elimination of waste products and in promoting the flow of urine, thereby speeding the removal of poisons from the liver. Green tea drinkers seldom suffer from kidney stones or other kidney ailments. However, if tea is drunk in overlarge quantities, or if it is made too strong, then the caffeine may overact and eliminate healthful as well as harmful substances from the body.

TANNIC ACID

Tannin combats alkaloid poisons and is an antidote to the harmful effects of consuming oily or fatty foods as it greatly stimulates digestion. Naturally it should not be ingested in great quantities, as happens when several cups of very strong tea are drunk. However, strong tea is of value on occasion, such as when needed to deal quickly and effectively with the effects of too much alcohol or rich food, and it is thought to give at least some help to those undergoing the painful symptoms of sudden withdrawal from nicotine or even heroin.

Tannic acid destroys various kinds of noxious bacteria and is, besides, an antidote to the effects of very hot weather. On the other hand, it corrodes metal; therefore teapots and kettles made of metals subject to corrosion should not be used.

VITAMINS A, B2, C, D AND P

Tea contains all these vitamins. It is sometimes said that vitamin C is destroyed during the processing of black tea, however, there is notable evidence to the contrary. The nomadic tribes of Mongolia and Central Asia live on an almost exclusively animal diet (meat and dairy products); their sole source of vitamin C comes from the large quantities of brick tea they consume. As brick tea is mainly manufactured from fully fermented tea, if the theory just mentioned were correct, the tribal people would have almost no intake of vitamin C at all. Since they appear to be extremely healthy as a race, one must suppose that at least some of this vitamin survives the process of fermentation. The individual effects of the vitamins mentioned here are widely known, so there is no need to say more on this subject.

A very small, but not negligible, amount of this substance is to be found in green and semi-fermented teas; in the processing of black teas it is unfortunately destroyed.

MANGANESE

The aromatic oils in tea have been found to play a part in calming the nerves, getting oxygen to the vital organs, and benefiting the circulatory system, besides stimulating the mind and the breathing process. As to this last point, several big cups of strong black tea, to which a largish quantity of sugar has been added, are said to have an almost immediate effect in reducing the discomforts caused by coughs, hoarseness or sore throats.

AROMATIC OILS

The Harmful Effects of Tea

The benign effects of tea are many; the harmful ones few. It seems obvious that tea does no harm at all to most people unless they drink it to excess, or make it very strong: matters that must be judged in the light of experience because of wide variations among individuals. What can be said with certainty is that, for health reasons, black tea should be drunk as soon as brewed; whereas the leaves of green and semi-fermented teas, though the flavour and aroma do not remain at their peak for a long time after brewing, can be left in the pot to 'stew' or undergo repeated rewatering at least for a few hours and still be wholesome and pleasant. Any tea regularly brewed overnight, left on the leaves and drunk the following morning can, however, be harmful. People who like morning tea but have no time to make it before rushing out to work should brew it at night and *strain it very thoroughly* before transferring it to a vacuum flask. Even so, small particles of tea leaves will get past the strainer so the freshly brewed tea should be transferred to the vacuum flask while still somewhat below the strength required, to allow for an all-night stewing of those particles.

CONTRA-
INDICATIONS
Tea should be avoided by those afflicted by insomnia or overexcitability.

Some Recent Medical Discoveries

Japanese doctors in particular, and others too, have been studying the beneficial effects of green tea. Some of the resulting indications are as follows:
1. Unfermented tea makes a valuable addition to the diet of convalescent patients;
2. It assists plane crews to keep alert during long flights;
3. It has slimming properties: some people have decreased their weight by several kilograms in half a year while remaining on a normal diet with the addition of plenty of green tea;
4. Its relatively high vitamin P content makes it beneficial in cases of high blood pressure and heart diseases;
5. According to newspaper reports, regular drinkers of green or oolong teas seldom fall victim to cancer. The modern Chinese tea books do not mention this, probably because the news is so recent.

The External Uses of Tea Leaves

MEDICAL USES
Very strong infusions of tea regularly used over a period of not less than several weeks for bathing the feet are often an effective cure for fungoid infections (such as 'Hong Kong foot') which have tenaciously resisted other treatment. Moreover, putting a layer of dried used tea leaves in every pair of socks kept in one's chest of drawers reduces the likelihood of reinfection.

Washing the face in tea left over from drinking cleanses the skin and causes the disappearance of various kinds of pimple and minor skin rash. In rural China, where medical aid was often out of reach, strong tea was found to be an effective, though mild, disinfectant for use on freshly incurred lacerations of the skin.

After washing the hair in the usual way, rinsing it thoroughly in strong tea makes it soft and glossy. This substitute for chemical shampoos, besides producing admirable results at virtually no cost, has none of the long-term side effects to be feared from chemical beauty aids.

Sufferers from halitosis or those who wish to cleanse their breath after consuming garlic, onions, leeks, etc. or alcohol, can banish offensive odours by keeping a few tea leaves in their mouths. In North China it was—and perhaps still is—the practice to rinse the mouth vigorously with strong tea immediately after every meal. This not only eliminates unpleasant odours but also detaches many of the food particles clinging to the teeth.

Toothache can sometimes be eased by gently chewing tea leaves or keeping them pressed against the affected tooth.

Tired eyes can be refreshed and caused to shine by bathing them in a weak infusion of green tea.

CULINARY USES

Tea eggs are tasty, and have an appetising colour and fragrance. First, lightly boil some eggs in ordinary water. Then, after gently cracking the shells, add plenty of used tea leaves to the water in the saucepan and boil them until hard enough to peel and slice.

Foods cured in tea smoke taste better than when other fuels are used for curing and have an appetising colour. The dyes used for food colouring may sometimes contain injurious ingredients, whereas strong tea may be safely used to produce an attractive reddish-brown colour.

OTHER USES

Used tea leaves contain carbohydrates, so they make a good manure for flowering plants, whether potted or growing in the earth. Rose bushes benefit prodigiously if used tea leaves are thrown daily onto the earth around their roots.

Newly purchased wooden furniture may smell unpleasantly of veneer, lacquer, etc. Washing in strong tea will remove the odour.

Garments made of silk and those made of rather similar synthetic materials will keep their colour and look fresh and glossy if washed in tea. The same is true of tatami or any kind of matting on which people walk, sit or sleep. In hot countries, where most people sleep on mats for the sake of coolness, the mats soon become impregnated with perspiration. Washing them in strong tea will remove the smell and make them look clean and new.

Burning tea leaves at dusk drives away mosquitoes. This can be done in one's bedroom about an hour before bedtime, using a metal trayful of smouldering leaves.

Used tea leaves accumulated day by day and thoroughly sun-dried can be used to stuff pillows. It is believed in China that people who use such pillows sleep well and wake up in the morning feeling clear-headed and in good spirits.

Some Personal Experiences

I have been drinking green or semi-fermented teas for the last fifty years. Normally I have a potful of hot, fresh tea made four to five times every day, using the finest green or semi-fermented kinds I can afford to buy. On the tray, together with the earthenware pot, are a small handleless cup and a beautiful bronze kettle for hot water. When I have enjoyed the flavour of the newly steeped tea, the tray is not removed. For here in this hot country (Thailand), I sip tea all day long, refilling the pot with water once or twice. If it were black tea, allowing water to remain on the leaves for hours at a time would make it undrinkable, but as it is either green or oolong tea, this stewing in tepid water does no harm. Naturally, the flavour diminishes and the aroma disappears after a while; nevertheless the cool tea drunk during the long intervals between the arrival of delicious hot tea is pleasantly refreshing, besides being enormously better for health than sweet, fizzy drinks.

Throughout my life I seem to have enjoyed almost every one of the benefits of tea mentioned above. I have been ill now and then, but not with any ailment that tea is believed to prevent, except for a fungoid infection between the toes of my left foot. Having only recently discovered in a Chinese tea book that bathing them daily in strong tea might clear up the infection, I have still to put that remedy to the test. For the rest, my circulatory, respiratory, digestive and excretory systems have seldom caused any trouble. For a man of seventy that record is not bad. Though this good fortune has surely not been solely due to regularly drinking quantities of green tea, one may assume that tea has played its part.

The Chinese as a race are dedicated eaters. It has been said that they know how to make every edible substance from earth, sky or sea taste delicious. Their frequent banquets are by no means light. True, the old 108-course banquets have long been out of fashion, and though the 16-, 24- or 32-course feasts common in China during the 1930s and 40s are rare in modern Thailand, one still gets invited very often to the eight-course kind, besides receiving presents on Chinese festival days of all kinds of special delicacies. Well, it might be thought that the Chinese would run to fat or be specially prone to digestive troubles, but in fact that is not so. Perhaps the reason is that they drink hot tea with each meal and also in between.

Chinese tea books say little about the effects of tea upon the human spirit beyond stating that it stimulates alertness and clear thinking. However, my own experience goes further. In this often hostile world, two people of disparate ages and different races who have never set eyes on one another are not likely to feel a mutual brotherly affection. Well, a year or so ago I had not as yet learnt of the existence of the Chinese author Yü Yü, who is now my tea brother. Chancing to come upon one of his tea books, I had an inspiration: 'Why, this is really excellent! How would it be to write something of the sort in English!' When I sent him a letter to ask if I might perhaps count upon his help in gathering materials, the reply was so extraordinarily friendly as to arouse my enthusiasm for what had been a tentative project. Further letters followed, and now we are like people who from the first meeting feel as though they had known each other from their cradles. But why should this happen to a couple who have never met? Because we are *tea people!* Chinese literature abounds in stories of men who became sworn brothers on the basis of a common love for tea, of for one or another of the arts characteristic of old China. This demonstrates the magical effects of sipping tea or playing the ancient lute in company with fellow votaries. I am sure that in this modern world where the pace of life is continually accelerating so that people get ulcers, dyspepsia, apoplexy and all kinds of mental ailment, practising the art of tea in the Chinese fashion is something well worth doing. As there are no hard and fast rules one may sit at ease on any kind of chair, on a cushion or on the grass, with no obligation to think or talk of this and that. Tea is conducive to full relaxation; and the more experience one is in the art of its carefree enjoyment, the truer this proves to be. Taking part in a tea session is a way of awakening to the Here and Now. To enjoy such subtle pleasures as the hiss and bubble of a kettle, the small white clouds of steam, the harmony of thoughtfully chosen utensils, the colour, flavour and aroma of the tea, one must resolutely banish cares (instead of allowing them to gnaw the mind like rats) and keep one's mind and senses focused on what lies to hand. This art, besides being delightful in itself, is a great deal cheaper than most other forms of therapy. I have yet to hear of regular tea people who need the help of professional analysts. To be a tea man or tea woman is to doctor one's mind. Cultivation of immediate responses to the Here and Now by means of the tea art leads gently to a more permanent awareness. Thereafter, the fragile beauties of each moment, which have hitherto been allowed to pass unnoticed, will receive our pleased attention. Thus we shall be guarded from preoccupation with a past already gone, or a future yet to come—a future that is likely to be less dismal than we feared if we know when and how to relax!

Postscript

Since completing this teabook, I have had two joyful experiences. In Grant Street, Chinatown, San Francisco, I discovered a new branch of the Ten Ren Tea Company lavishly stocked with fine teas (and some teapots, etc.). This I take to be an omen of the growing availability in the West of oolong and green teas.

In Taiwan I recently came face to face with Yü-Yü, my Tea Brother. His welcome included a visit to a teahouse beautifully furnished in Chinese traditional style, where superb teas are prepared at the customers' tables by young ladies with a thorough mastery of every nuance of the Chinese art of tea. I am told that most cities in Taiwan have a few good teahouses of this kind.

Appendices

Unfortunately, there is no way of romanising Chinese so that people unacquainted with the language can pronounce all the words correctly. In this book I have used the Wade-Giles system prevalent in Taiwan and formerly employed almost universally. The following table gives Wade-Giles, the new mainland China system and approximate English equivalents.

Wade-Giles	Mainland China	English Equivalent
ch	j,zh	j
ch'	ch,q	ch
hs	x	ch
j	r	r
k	g	g
k'	k	k
p	b	b
p'	p	p
t	d	d
t'	t	t
ts	z	d
tsê	ze	dze(r)
tś	c	t
ts'ê	ce	tse(r)
tzŭ	zi	dz
ts'ŭ	ci	ts
ieh	ie	yeh
ien	ian	ien
ih	i	rr
ung	ong	ung (vowel as in 'put')

Vowels not listed here resemble Latin, Spanish and Italian vowels. Consonants not listed here (whether in Wade-Giles or Mainland China) resemble English consonants.

My hyphenation throughout this book may be slightly erratic but can be largely explained by a single example, Li Chi-Lan. Li is a surname; Chi-Lan is a personal name. In other words, the hyphen denotes a specially close connection between two words. However, I have invariably used hyphens to join the syllables of Chinese tea names and given both syllables capitals to make all of them uniform.

Note that for a few words which have been used by English tea merchants for centuries the traditional but inaccurate English spellings have been retained: namely oolong, keemun, bohea and suchong.

Names of Some Available Teas

Here I am providing names of teas in both old and new spellings so as to facilitate purchase. As noted in Appendix 1, the romanised spelling of Chinese words now officially adopted in mainland China differs considerably from the Wade-Giles spelling hitherto used both internationally and elsewhere in this book. In the following table, 'old spelling' denotes Wade-Giles; 'new spelling' denotes the mainland China system.

MAINLAND TEAS

English name	Old spelling (Wade-Giles)	New Spelling (mainland)	Type
Dragon's Well	Lung-Ching	Long-Jing	green
Lion's Peak	Shih-Fêng	Shi-Feng	green
White Cloud	Pai-Yün	Bai-Yun	green
Jewelled Cloud	Pao-Yün	Bao-Yun	green
Purple Sprout	Tz'ê-Sun	Ce-Sun	green
Old Man's Eyebrows	Shou-Mei	Shou-Mei	green
Iron Goddess of Mercy	T'ieh-Kuan-Yin	Tie-Guan-Yin	oolong*
Iron Arahan	T'ieh-Lo-Han	Tie-Lo-Han	oolong
Water Fairy (Iris)	Shui-Hsien	Shui-Xian	oolong
Paper Packed	Pao-Chung	Bao-Zhong	oolong
Small or Cut Leaves	Hsiao-Chung	Xiao-Zhong	oolong
Sparrow Tongue	Ch'iao-Shê	Qiao-Shê	oolong
Dragon Phoenix*	Lung-Fêng	Long-Fêng	oolong
Dragon-Garden Pearl	Lung-Yüan-Chu	Long-Yuan-Zhu	oolong
Real Dragon Shoots	Chêng-Lung-Ya	Zhêng-Long-Ya	oolong
keemun	Ch'i-Mên	Qi-Men	red (black)
Fukien Red	Min-Hung	Min-Hong	red (black)
P'u-Êrh	P'u-Êrh	Pu-Er	white, green or red (black)

*'Oolong' is here used in a broad sense to cover all partly fermented teas, including the very lightly fermented kind properly called 'bohea' in English.

*Dragon-phoenix, dragon-garden-pearl and real-dragon-shoots are not mentioned in the text of this book, as these three high quality export teas were previously unknown to me.

Green tea	Ch'ing-Ch'a		– green	
Dragon's Well (style)	Lung-Chung (style)		– green	
Tung-Ting	Tung-Ting		– oolong	
Oolong (style)	Wu-Lung		– green or oolong	
water fairy (iris)	Shui-Hsien		– oolong	
Paper-Packed	Pao-Chung		– oolong	
Bright-Virtue	Ming-Tê		– oolong	
Coniferous Evergreen	Sung-Po-Ch'ing		– green	
Harbour Tea	Kang-Kou		– oolong	
Iron Goddess of Mercy (style)	T'ieh-Kuan-Yin		– oolong	

				FLOWER TEAS MAINLAND OR TAIWAN
A general name	Hua-Ch'a	Hua-cha	Mostly red (black)	
A general name	Hsiang-P'ien	Xiang-Pian	Mostly red (black)	
jasmine tea	Mo-Li	Mo-Li	Mostly red (black)	
chrysanthemum tea	Chu-Hua	Ju-Hua	Any kind of leaf	

Names of Cities and Provinces Mentioned in the Text

To complicate matters still further, I have felt obliged to use yet a third system of romanisation for the more widely known cities and provinces, namely the system hitherto used almost universally on atlases throughout the world; for those are the spellings with which the huge majority of readers are likely to be familiar. The following table gives the atlas spellings first, then the Wade-Giles system of romanisation and finally the new mainland romanisation.

Ch'ang-An, the T'ang dynasty capital, is now known as Si-An.

Atlas	Wade-Giles	Mainland China
Cities		
Canton	Kuang-Chou	Guangzhou
Chang-An	Ch'ang-An	Changan
Chengtu	Ch'êng-tu	Chengdu
Chingteh	Ching-tê	Jingde
Chungking	Ch'ung-Ching	Chongquing
Hangchow	Hang-Chou	Hangzhow
I-Hsing	I-Hsing	Yixing
Kanhsien	Kan-Hsien	Ganxian
Kweichow	Kwei-Chou	Guizhou
Nanking	Nan-Ching	Nanjing
Peking	Pei-Ching	Beijing
Shanghai	Shang-hai	Shanghai
Si-An	Si-an	Xian
Soochow	Su-chou	Suzhou
Tientsin	T'ien-Ching	Tianjing

Provinces

Anhwei	An-hui	Anhui
Chekiang	Chê-chiang	Zhejiang
Fukien	Fu-chien	Fujian
Hunan	Hu-nan	Hunan
Kiangsi	Chiang-hsi	Jiangxi
Kiangsu	Chiang-su	Jiangsu
Kwangtung or Kuangtung	Kuang-tung	Guangdong
Szechuan or Szechwan	Szê-chuan	Sichuan
Taiwan	T'ai-wan	Taiwan
Yunnan	Yun-nan	Yunnan

CHINA'S MAIN TEA-PRODUCING PROVINCES

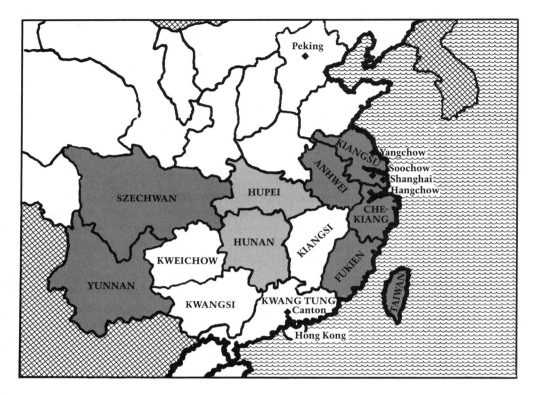

Provinces famous for their teas
Less important tea-growing provinces
All provinces named on this map produce some tea.

Ch'a-shih-ch'un-ch'iu, by Yü-Yü (Taipei)
Ch'a-shih-ch'a-hua, by Yü-Yü (Taipei)
Ch'a-hsueh-man-hua, by Chang T'ieh-Chün (Taipei)
Ch'a-shih-ch'a-tien, by Chu Hsiao-Ming (Taipei)
Ch'a-tien, by Ch'ên Hsiang (Taipei)
Yin-ch'a-man-hua, by Zhuang-Man-Feng (Peking)
                    Kong Xian-Lo
                    Tang Li-Xin
                    Wang Qia-Sheng

Illustrations Photographs not otherwise acknowledged are from the author's collection

The window and balustrade lattices used throughout the book are drawn from Chinese teahouses, teashops, residences, and Buddhist and Taoist temples. The oldest design dates from the Han dynasty; the most recent is nineteenth century. Courtesy Dover Publications, Inc., New York, from *Chinese Lattice Designs* by Daniel Sheets Dye.

Incidental illustrations are drawn from Chinese sources. Courtesy Nam San Publisher, Hong Kong, from *Chinese Art of Designs,* by Yee Nam San.